MW00608189

This book is not about making you a leader…

It's intended to give you critical insights that you'll need to survive and thrive in the *new normal* we find ourselves in today.

As businesses rethink the future of work and reinvent their workplaces and people, they will require a reimagined leader.

In the way we lead, real transformation is essential.

LEADERSHIP REIMAGINED

The Future Of Leadership Has Arrived

We are at a Disruption Point
Requiring a Workplace,
Workforce, and Leaders with a
Different Composition

-R. F. Price

LEADERSHIP REIMAGINED

The Future Of Leadership Has Arrived

Absolute Author
Publishing House

Leadership Reimagined

Want to buy a lot of these books? Great. We can help. Please contact us at orders@understandingleadership.org for more information.

Copyright 2021 by Robert F. Price

The views expressed in this book are those solely of the author and do not reflect the position of any person, place, entity, or organization and is not meant to express or imply any association or endorsement as such.

Limit of Liability/Disclaimer of Warranty: While the publisher and author have used their best efforts in preparing this book, they make no representation or warranties with respect to the accuracy or completeness of all the contents of this book and specifically disclaim any implied warranties of merchantability or fitness for a particular purpose. No warranty may be created or extended by sales representatives or written sales material. The advice and strategies contained herein may not be suitable for your situation. You should consult with a professional where appropriate. Neither the publisher nor author shall be liable for any loss of profit or any commercial damages, including but not limited to special, incidental, consequential, or other damages.

Notice to Readers: Be aware that Internet Web sites offered as citations and/or sources for more information may have changed or discontinued between the time this was written and when it was read.

Trade Paperback ISBN 978-1-64953-306-7

All rights reserved. No part of this book may be reproduced or transmitted in any form by any means, electronic or mechanical, including photocopying and recording, or by any information storage or retrieval system without permission in writing from the author.

Published in the United States by Absolute Author Publishing House
New Orleans, LA

Institute for the Study of Leadership
www.understandingleadership.org
Printed in the United States of America
2021

Publisher in Chief Melissa Caudle, Ph.D.
Editor Johnson Mesio
Cover Layout Design by ProDesign X
Interior Design by
Author's Photograph by Julia Kimbrell Photography

20 21 22 23 24 5 4 3 2 1

"

I learned as an army officer how to keep a combat unit together, after they've risked and lost so much... how to ask them to travel further with me, not knowing if they'll survive. It's a lesson that reminds me that everything we do as leaders matters every decision, every action.

"

- R.F. Price

The Bottom-Line Up Front

The Bottom Line for you to successfully adapt to the new normal and become a Reimagined Leader.

When I was attending the U.S. Army Officer's Candidate School to earn my commission, I spent all night learning a lesson that I've never forgotten about leadership: *"The people that suffer the most from my inability to adhere to the standards are my subordinates."* I literally spent all night one hot-summer's night in Georgia chanting that phrase repeatedly over and over again, while doing a duck walk up and down a military barracks hallway.

If you don't adapt to the changes our current conditions require, not only will your people suffer, but your organization will too as the most talented people in your company may leave in droves to work somewhere else because of your inability to lead in the new normal.

There are two main challenges at the root of the problem that you must overcome to be a successful hybrid workplace leader today: the issues are *trust* (or the lack of trust you have for your people) and *control* (or your fear of losing it and your inability to manage beyond what you can see).

The solution centers on a concept I call **People** = Human Factor.

As a Reimagined Leader, you'll need to embrace it and master the competencies it requires. The power of *"people squared"* is doubling down on the emotional, the human elements, of how people feel and how you connect with them as a leader.

Don't underestimate the world we live in today – the new normal. The Employee Value Proposition (EVP) has changed. Executives talk about organization culture and the importance of maintaining it. People hear control, i.e., "You want me back in the office so you can see me." Executives counter with the importance to maintain the health of the company and its lifeblood (culture), but people aren't interested in the attributes at work they once were. People no longer care about working for the next Google in their industry. Those ancillary things like free soda, coffee bars, doughnut socials, pizza lunches, cool t-shirts, and company sponsored events have become invaluable trinkets and more of an inconvenience. As senior leaders move to "get back to the old normal" and offer social activities with the best of intentions, people feel obligated, not motivated to participate. The attributes organizations provided as perks, often costly by the way, aren't what people want now.

The pandemic disruption caused people to look at their priorities and work much differently. If you surveyed employee's pre-pandemic and asked what they wanted in a company's culture, you would have heard feedback like: family atmosphere, social, fun.

Now it's flexibility is king. Let me choose how, where, and when I get my work completed. I've proven I can do it for more than a year now. It triumph's everything employers thought they knew about culture.

We're still in a global pandemic potentially contending with variants and a retraction of freedoms and even a loss of the progress that's been made. Even as this book finishes the final edit process, most of America's Midwest and Southern states are back in the red with the return of masks looming for both the vaccinated and unvaccinated. The pandemic is not over – it's not over until it's over… as they say.

There's a much larger issue we all face: **BURNOUT**.

Relentless contention with threats against our own and our family's health and safety, the psychological affects of extended periods of separation and isolation as adults and for our children, the stress of adapting to new norms of life and work, work that often never ends at home as professionals, spouses, and parents.

The human factor is the real deal. Lead with empathy and acknowledge emotions.

When was the last time you asked a member of your team how they're feeling?

CONTENTS

PREFACE..1

INTRODUCTION..2

PART I: WHAT GOT US HERE, WON'T GET US THERE 9

CHAPTER 1: LEADERSHIP: THE WAY WE WERE 10

PART II: THE HYBRID LEADERSHIP TSUNAMI............................. 33

CHAPTER 2: THE GLOBAL PANDEMIC: EVERYTHING CHANGED 34

PART III: SURVIVING THE SHOCK WAVE & WAKE 55

CHAPTER 3: CHALLENGES THE NEW NORMAL CREATES FOR LEADERS..... 56

PART IV: RESHAPING THE NATURE OF WORK & THE WORKPLACE 77

CHAPTER 4: LEADING A THRIVING HYBRID ECOSYSTEM...................... 78

CHAPTER V: LEADING A THRIVING HYBRID ECOSYSTEM 99

CHAPTER FIVE: LEADING A THRIVING HYBRID ECOSYSTEM 100

NOTES.. 122

Preface

A t one point in time, companies acquiring the right knowledge worker were seen as the organizations with the greatest competitive advantage of the era.

During the global epidemic and in the following months of the wake created by COVID-19, companies face a new challenge. The companies that will survive and thrive in our current climate of social balancing and workforce adaption to the "blended work-life," along with preparing for the next set of business, environmental, and social challenges are those companies willing and eager to change.

A progression from the contemporary philosophy of work-life balance, the separation of work and personal life, to the current condition of blended-life balance, whereby people work and live on their own terms, not by a conventional timeclock or calendar.

The advantage will be for those companies that attract, cultivate, and retain leaders with the necessary skills to lead in a hybrid work environment.

Leaders with a different composition of skills. More authentic, transparent, and empathetic leaders.

It's a new day and new time demanding new leaders.

Why would we ever return to the way things were? Your people won't!

The time is now for Leadership Reimagined.

Introduction

B efore the big blow of the coronavirus, leadership structures in the United States and worldwide have undergone constant change since the Industrial Revolution. Rapid technological transformation and the expansion of digitized gadgets and services have accompanied human development in recent decades. As a result, leadership had remained autocratic until recently, when it began to observe a dramatic shift in how operations are managed in today's corporate environment.

There's no doubting that the COVID-19 outbreak has changed the corporate landscape dramatically. In 2020, many businesses lost twenty to sixty percent of their revenue, and more than fourteen million Americans lost their employment, either temporarily or permanently.

Every sector and facet of life has been affected by the pandemic. As we all rushed to adjust quickly, 2020 was a year of a drastic shift in strategies and policy. With ongoing concerns about health and safety, job security, disruptions in schooling, and financial constraints, it's clear that we can't overlook the emotional consequences. In the way we lead, real transformation is essential.

Our perception of great leadership has historically been defined by rigorous delegation and direction, with managers leading the way and employees follow suit. This perception has developed as we continue to deal with disruptions in our organizations and personal lives, as managers who have remained effective have recognized a shift in what new leadership demands. We need to rethink how we lead and redefine what it means to be strong. COVID-19 has introduced a new template that we should use when hiring managers and leaders. Those with advanced "soft skills" will be the ones who lead our companies into the future.

In difficult times, the world has looked to its leaders for inspiration and advice on solving complex problems. Many remarkable leaders have motivated millions of people worldwide to change the world for the better.

However, the rapid pace of commercial and technological change that has characterized the twenty-first century has resulted in significant changes in virtually every industry. The fast-paced global corporate environment has bred a new generation of leaders who feel that employee professional development is the key to organizational success.

Because of the pandemic, leadership has become more collaborative, and people oriented. It's hard to comprehend that the autocratic rule was the norm until a few decades ago. When managers made key decisions with little to no involvement from their staff since remote working was an abstract concept. The emphasis was on completing work, a replication of the production model birthed in the age of industrial revolution.

Many businesses have grasped the benefits of allowing employees to work from home, and as a result, some global workforces may never set foot in an office again. According to the PwC US Pulse Survey, fifty-four percent of CFOs want to make remote work a permanent option for their organizations. As a result, managers may have to figure out how to manage partially remote teams shortly.

Technological and commercial breakthroughs and disruptions have shaped today's world. Since change is inevitable in all business disciplines, strong leadership has become more adaptable and flexible. Employee involvement is frequently considered crucial to decision-making processes, and employee engagement is a key human resource management tenet.

Organizations have dismantled barriers and broken down silos in ways that no one could have predicted. They've streamlined choices and processes, empowered frontline leaders, and put a stop to bureaucracy and hierarchies that move slowly. Hence, the rise of remote working choices has shaped leadership as we know it, especially in these times. Because micromanagement is difficult in remote situations, confidence in employees has become a key aspect of the leadership shift.

Empowerment is at the heart of modern leadership. It was a common misconception during the Industrial Revolution that most workers couldn't think for themselves. They required a leader with more intelligence and expertise to direct their actions. When work changed from physical labor to white-collar jobs, this directive form of human resource management fell out of favor.

A more integrative leadership approach is used in modern teams. Employee productivity is determined by understanding the desired outcomes and the availability of the necessary conditions and resources.

Leaders in today's world are frequently enablers rather than managers. They recognize an employee's capabilities and provide all necessary resources to use those strengths to achieve the best possible results.

Leaders of today are active participants. Earlier types of leadership relied heavily on job delegation, with managers' responsibilities mostly consisting of allocating tasks to various teams and monitoring their progress. Even though delegation is still a key aspect of leadership, today's managers and leaders are considerably more invested in their teams and businesses. They take on additional responsibilities such as training and mentoring to steer their teams through key projects and to help them develop their talents.

When discussing the complexity of leadership in recent times, introducing a sense of community is also worth addressing. Today's corporate environments are made up of small, close-knit communities. Today's leaders are professionally and personally closer to their teams, thanks to Human Resource (HR) initiatives such as team activities and greater connections.

Technology's ongoing evolution has had an impact on all key domains, including leadership. Leaders used to rush to stay on top of their communications with external and internal stakeholders just a few years ago. Managers couldn't see completed assignments in real-time without quick emails and phone calls. They also lost negotiating leverage with outside parties since news would arrive days after making choices.

Leaders may use modern technology to create more collaborative work environments and give their employees more freedom to execute their jobs. It has also allowed modern managers to bring in extra resources as and when they are needed to complete large projects.

The rate at which technology and business change will only accelerate in the future, the concept of effective leadership will also continue to evolve. As a result, investing in leadership development and understanding organizational development will be critical to advancing the corporate world.

Despite the favorable turnaround and tremendous improvements, corporate inequality and social injustices continue to plague the workplace. Global structural inequality based on gender, race, class, handicap, and ethnicity has been revealed, fed off, and escalated by the pandemic, which has been compounded and complicated by today's difficulties.

The world has prospered in recent decades as a result of digitization. People are living longer and healthier lives on average. The rise of a global middle class has been fueled by rapid economic expansion in emerging economies. Despite this, poverty and inequality continue to exist. Wealth is concentrated, and income-earning prospects and educational and healthcare standards are widely disparate.

These inequities stifle economic progress and human development while increasing vulnerability to pandemics, economic crises, and climate change - all of which can quickly destabilize nations.

With the pandemic threatening the largest rise in inequality since records began, leaders from all sectors must achieve social justice, recognizing and correcting underlying disparities a top priority. As a result, leaders must reinvent, disband, and reorganize pre-COVID norms and institutions. To achieve fairness in the workspace, leaders must consciously strike a nail in the coffin of the ideology that enabled and accelerated the current level of inequality.

As leaders begin to stage the return to work, instead of attempting a return to business as usual, they have the opportunity to rethink the workplace by leveraging new insights and advancements generated over the preceding several months. To effectively lead these teams in a post-pandemic workplace, leaders need to develop a new set of skills to survive and thrive in the new normal.

PART I

What Got Us Here, Won't Get Us There

Chapter 1

Leadership: The Way We Were

The Bottom Line: Leaders must change their approach to planning, scheduling, and monitoring tasks and performance based on results, not activity.

What Got Us Here?

There have been individuals who have sought to figure out how and why leaders have been effective for as long as there have been leaders. Although leadership has not changed, our understanding of it has. It's critical to comprehend why very diverse leadership styles can be effective, why the same leadership approaches won't work in every situation, and which leadership style is most suited to your personality. Everyone has leadership potential but grasping these concepts can help you reach your full potential as a leader.

Simply put, "leadership" refers to "the ability to lead." Regrettably, this isn't useful. According to the BNET online Business Dictionary, leadership is, "The power to provide direction and to influence and align others toward a common objective, motivating and committing them to action, and holding them accountable for their performance." This is more descriptive, but it isn't significant. It does not define leadership, but rather what it accomplishes.

There have been leaders throughout history. We are social beings that form bonds with one another, yet we also want order amid life's chaos. We want to be organized so that we can accomplish goals as a society that we can't do alone. As a result, someone has to be in charge at some point.

In the past, leaders were classified into one of three groups: political, military, or religious.

Around 1790 B.C., Babylonian Political ruler Hammurabi compiled laws, which unified his empire in what was viewed as a fair system because everyone was bound by the same set of rules.

Sun Tzu was a Chinese military leader who lived around 500 B.C. Although he was a great military leader, he created the Art of War, which is about how to avoid deploying armies except as a last resort, focusing instead on sensible political policies and techniques to avoid war.

Religious leaders may be said to have had the greatest impact on their civilizations, with consequences that have lasted for generations.

The rise of the industrial revolution ushered in a new breed of leader: the economic leader. Instead of swords, the so-called Captains of

Industry discovered they could construct an empire using modern technologies. Without the aid of armies, oil barons, railroad magnates, and factory owners amassed vast riches, sometimes at the expense of the people they employed. As a result, Union leaders and diverse initiatives arose to promote justice in areas where violations were suspected.

Scientists now had easy access to a wide range of new materials for their study, which expanded the number of Scientific Leaders during the Industrial Revolution. Psychiatry and psychology rose to prominence as a result of studies on workplace productivity and its impact on the workforce.

Workers are more productive when they work in a "good work environment," according to studies. The boss's attitude and influence have a significant role in this productivity. Employees who believe they are listened to, respected, and treated fairly at work are happier and perform better than those who feel disrespected and underappreciated. Which type of workplace would you prefer?

Frederick Winslow Taylor introduced scientific management in the early twentieth century. This isn't a leadership philosophy per such, but it revolutionized the way leaders and managers engaged with employees and managed product production. Taylor understood that employers could get the most out of their workers if they separated labor projects into their numerous sections and trained laborers to specialize in each particular station of production based on their own work experience and informal education. Taylor timed each step of the manufacturing process to ensure optimal efficiency. When it came to organizational leadership, Taylor felt that leaders were born, not manufactured and that there was only one way to lead effectively. We will learn later in this book that this assumption is erroneous.

Leadership Theories and Management Approaches

In every organization, leadership is a critical function. Without a leader, no organization can exist. Any organization's goal is determined by the people who are employed to pursue the organization's goals. Sound leadership that can influence personnel in such a way that they all aspire to achieve the organization's ultimate goal is critical to effective administration. Importantly, employees should be encouraged to work eagerly and confidently. Given the importance of leadership in an organization, it is necessary to explore many theories regarding leadership and leaders that have been investigated by several experts.

Effective leadership is widely acknowledged as critical to any organization's success. There has been a movement in the recognition of the value of human capital and organizational management. But what's the difference between management and leadership? Managers monitor and regulate performance, preserving order and stability in an organization, whereas leaders are considered as visionaries and strategists. Some scholars think that leaders and managers have separate duties and responsibilities, while others say that leadership and management are complementary and that separating them in practice would be difficult. to gain a better grasp of the concept of leadership, It is necessary to trace the historical development of the key leadership theories and analyze the progress made over time in order. It looks at four different eras of leadership theory: trait, behavioral, situational, and new.

Trait era: Great Man theory (the 1840s) and trait theories (the 1930s–1940s)

The focus of leadership study in the nineteenth century was on discovering the personality traits and other features of good leaders, as well as the innate characteristics of a leader. The Great Man theory's central tenet is that leaders are born, not manufactured or schooled. In other words, only a select few, extremely uncommon individuals are endowed with the qualities necessary to be good leaders and achieve greatness by divine design. Popular historical individuals such as Julius Caesar, Mahatma Gandhi, Abraham Lincoln, and Napoleon Bonaparte were frequently used as examples. These people were thought to be natural-born leaders having inherent leadership qualities that enabled them to lead others while shaping history.

The characteristic hypotheses arose from the Great Man theory. Leaders can be born or made, according to trait theories. In other words, successful leadership attributes can be inherited or learned via training and practice. The goal was to find the optimal mix of characteristics that create a good leader, with a focus on leaders' mental, social, and physical features. However, no consistent set of qualities was developed, and by 1950, it looked that continuing with this technique would be futile, therefore it was abandoned. Psychometric instruments, which are frequently employed in staff recruitment, are an illustration of trait theory ideas in operation today. These techniques are used to improve personal performance and team growth by highlighting crucial personality qualities.

Behavioral era: behavioral theory (the 1940s–1950s)

The behavioral view, which emerged from trait theories, says that leaders are mostly formed, not born, and that good leadership can be learned. It focuses on the leader's actual actions rather than their attributes or characteristics, yet it generally ignores the leader's circumstances and environment.

Different patterns of conduct have been classified and identified as styles as a result of research in this field. Blake and Mouton's Managerial Grid is likely the best-known example of this approach in management training. This view is now exemplified by an abundance of leadership-development programs that focus on the development of leadership abilities and behaviors, bolstering the belief that leadership is mostly learned.

Situational era: contingent and situational theories (the 1960s)

The importance of the environment in the leader-follower relationship was eventually acknowledged, and this notion dominated the situational age. The situational period, as the name implies, is focused on leadership in specific situations rather than on leadership attributes or behaviors. This means that leaders must be able to assess the environment in which they work and then determine which leadership style will best 'fit' the scenario. The contingency theory of leadership is named after the fact that the best style depends on the context.

One of the first contingency theories of leadership was proposed by Fred Fiedler. His thesis emphasizes the relevance of context in poor leadership and backs up the idea that there is no one-size-fits-all set of leadership characteristics or activities. Fiedler, on the other hand, believes that because a leader's style is permanent, they should be placed in situations that best suit their personality. In other words, a leader's efficacy is defined by how well their leadership style fits a certain situation.

New leadership era: transactional, transformational theories (the 1990s) and others (the 2000s)

For the first time, it was understood that focusing on just one feature or dimension of leadership would not be sufficient to address the phenomenon's complexity. 16 A demand for leadership theories that enable rapid change, disruptive technology innovation, and increased globalization has evolved in a society that has become more complicated and challenging. This ushered in a new era of leadership, moving away from the old theories of leadership, which characterize leadership as a top-down, unidirectional influencing process that draws a clear boundary between leaders and followers. Rather, the attention shifted to the complicated interconnections between the leader, the followers, the situation, and the environment. Instead, the focus shifted to the complex interconnections between the leader, the followers, the circumstance, and the system as a whole, with special attention paid to the followers' latent leadership abilities.

Transactional and Transformational Theories

The aforementioned background aided the popularity and implementation of two leadership theories: transformational and transactional theories, as well as methodologies like the Lean strategy and agile methodology to deal with the quick pace of change and increasing complexity of the difficulties addressed.

Leaders that practice transformational leadership encourage, inspire, and motivate their followers. When an organization needs to be reinvigorated, is through considerable change, or requires a new direction, this approach is applied. It is especially important in today's fast-paced technological economy, where agility and innovation may make or break a company. It's especially important in today's fast-paced technological business, where agility and innovation may make or ruin a company. Jeff Bezos, Steve Jobs, and Bill Gates are all examples of transformational leaders.

On the other side, transactional leadership focuses on authority to encourage personnel. The leader rewards followers for their efforts and punishes those who do not accomplish their objectives. In this setting, the follower's view of the exchange with the leader's fairness and equity is critical. To keep mature businesses on track and support the status quo, transactional leadership works best in mature firms with clearly defined structures and goals. Managers, for example, are transactional leaders that prioritize oversight, processes, and follower performance.

The creation of shared, collective, and collaborative leadership approaches resulted from the ongoing shift in leadership paradigms. According to them, an organization's performance is more dependent on distributed coordinative leadership methods rather than the activities of a few individuals at the top. Servant leadership resurfaced as a popular concept, emphasizing the value of followers. Servant leaders are mainly concerned with serving people first, and they endeavor to help their team members. Inclusive leadership, which emphasizes a person-centered approach, has lately evolved. It is focused on the dynamic processes that take place between leaders and followers, and it focuses on encouraging followers to take on leadership roles. Finally, complexity leadership arose as a way to deal with the complexity of our modern world, and it is included in contemporary leadership theory. This theory considers contextual interactions that occur across an entire social system from a whole system perspective.

Leadership ideology is a vibrant, dynamic entity that evolves with time. It has been thoroughly researched over time, and numerous theories have evolved. Traditional leadership theories include the Great Man theory, which holds that a leader is born to lead and hence possesses certain innate attributes that make them suitable for the position. Trait theory, which is derived from the Great Man hypothesis, states that leaders can be born or produced and that an effective leader requires a mix of specific attributes. The behavioral theory followed, claiming that leaders are primarily chosen based on their deeds rather than their psychological attributes. The importance of environmental influences was soon recognized, and contingency and situational theories were added to the mix. Following the modern era, there was a change away from an emphasis on leaders and their characteristics and toward considering the complex and ongoing interactions and interrelationships between the leader, the followers, and the situation. Shared communal and collaborative leadership, as well as inclusive leadership, are among the theories that have resulted. Finally, complexity leadership evolved, which focuses on an organization's entire system.

Examining the evolution of leadership theories across time provides some needed perspective as well as a background in which to grasp the subject's complexity. Each theory has advantages and disadvantages, and each appears to supply a piece of the leadership puzzle. Organizations are always coping with change and uncertainty in today's complex, dynamic, and globalized environment, and no one, no theory, has been able to handle all of the leadership problems. Given the complexity of our modern environment, many people believe that old hierarchical notions of leadership are becoming less and less relevant. This resulted in a change in emphasis away from the traits and behaviors of leaders and toward a more systemic view of leadership as a collective social process resulting from various elements interacting. In an attempt to deal with the changing realities of organizations and businesses, new leadership theories were developed, resulting in newer and more relevant definitions of leader, follower, and circumstance.

Moving from Good to Great: (An Old Model or Approach)

Fannie Mae was losing $1 million every business day when David Maxwell took over as CEO in 1981, with $56 billion in mortgage loans underwater. The board was eager to learn WHAT Maxwell planned to do to save the company. Maxwell, being a visionary, recognized that the board was off to a bad start. He told them, "That's the wrong first question," as all great leaders do in response to the "what" query. Trying to figure out where you want to take the firm before you have the right people in place and the wrong people out is a bad idea.

Maxwell advised his management team that the company would only hire A-level employees who were willing to put in A-plus effort. He spoke with every member of the team. He told them all the same thing: it was going to be a long and difficult journey. If they didn't want to go, that's great; just let them know. He stated that now is the moment to exit the vehicle. There were no questions asked, and there were no repercussions. In total, fourteen of the company's twenty-six executives were fired. They were replaced by some of the industry's best, sharpest, and hardest-working executives.

Maxwell devoted his entire focus to the "what" question after ensuring that the right individuals were in the right place at the right time. Fannie Mae went from losing $1 million per day at the beginning of its term to earning $4 million per day in the end. Even after Maxwell's departure in 1991, his outstanding team continued to turn the flywheel, and Fannie Mae achieved cumulative stock returns roughly eight times higher than the general market from 1984 to 1999.

Every business is similar to a vehicle. Unless pushed and driven well, it is without the ability to move forward or backward. As a result, it is the responsibility of a great leader to get it started. As a result, as a leader, you must decide where you're going, how you'll get there, and who will accompany you. Most people believe that outstanding leaders begin their journey by announcing their destination to the rest of the company—by charting a new course or articulating a new corporate vision.

Leaders of firms that progress from good to great begin with "who," not "where." They begin by getting the correct people on board, the incorrect people off the board, and the correct people in the correct seats. And no matter how bad things go, they cling to their discipline—first the people, then the direction.

Good-to-great leaders grasp three key realities when it comes to getting started. First, starting with "who" allows you to more quickly adjust to a rapidly changing world. If people board your bus because they think it's going somewhere, you'll have a problem when you get ten miles down the road and realize you need to change directions because the world has changed. However, if people board the vehicle mostly because of the other excellent people on board, you will be far faster and smarter in adapting to changing circumstances. Second, if your organization has the appropriate personnel, you won't have to worry about motivating them. The appropriate people are self-motivated: There's nothing like being part of a team that's expected to provide outstanding outcomes. Finally, nothing else matters if you have the wrong people in your firm. Even if you're on the right track, you won't be able to accomplish greatness. With mediocre personnel and great vision, you'll get mediocre results.

It's also worth noting that it's amazing leadership, not a management team, that elevates an organization from mediocre to great. This takes us to the distinction between management and leadership. There is also a distinction to be made between leadership and great leadership. It's important to remember that leaders and managers differ in several key areas.

Management is concerned with the day-to-day implementation of plans, but leadership is concerned with establishing a vision and then putting it into action through a sense of mission. Of course, leaders must be outstanding managers as well, because leadership is as much about having a Twenty Thousand Feet vision as it is about putting plans into action on the ground.

The main difference between leadership and management, however, is that leaders must be transformational personalities who can inspire and persuade their followers to buy into their vision for the greater benefit of the race. Managers require this as well, although it is primarily for ad hoc management and microtask execution. Similarly, there are distinctions between traditional leaders and transformational leaders. While all businesses, nations, and societies have many leaders, there are only a few times in history when genuinely remarkable and transformational leaders appear on the global stage.

While every business has a stable of leaders, only a few organizations have the opportunity to experience revolutionary leadership. Why, for example, did Microsoft and Apple grow into such massive behemoths while smaller technological companies continue to post record profits but are not mentioned in the same breath? The distinction is that both Microsoft and Apple were formed by very extraordinary individuals (Bill Gates and Steve Jobs, respectively) who not only had a vision but were also ready to put their reputations on the line to make that vision a reality. Furthermore, due to the caliber and potential of both Microsoft and Apple, both companies were incredibly imaginative and ingenious of Gates and Jobs.

As a result, leadership and transformative leadership are two distinct characteristics that must be taken into account if one wants to understand why not all businesses reach greatness from a good position. The old paradigm usually ensured that the leader led and the masses followed. The leader was in charge; he or she made the decisions. There was no one to discuss with, so the leader was mostly on his own. The closest counsel was weeks or months away, and the success of whatever project you were on hinged on the leader's sound judgment and self-assurance.

However, the leader's capacity to inspire those who followed him was equally crucial. For instance, there are several accounts of Roman Emperors being assassinated by their troops once they lost faith in them. There have been several CEOs who have experienced the same fate after their stockholders lost faith in them. It was essentially a military paradigm, and until the Industrial Revolution, it was our only genuine leadership model. Even if the leadership style was flawless, it could not change a decent firm or organization into a great one.

The world was still essentially split into leaders and employees until the turn of the century, and it was a very orderly place. However, something has changed in the business world in the previous two decades. With the arrival of the machines, ushering in the first industrial revolution, leadership began to take on a new shape, becoming more employee centered. They recognize that bringing in the proper personnel will undoubtedly propel the company's padders from good to exceptional.

Evolution of Work

Work is changing, which means that new technology and behaviors are entering our workplaces. The consumer web is primarily to blame for these new behaviors and technology, and businesses are now scrambling to adapt. The workplace is changing at a breakneck pace. Employers, regardless of geography or industry, will need to be aware of – and manage – five underlying themes to lead and flourish in the future. Employees' demands for more choice and flexibility, as well as access to real-time learning, enhanced autonomy, stability, and the ability to engage on personally important projects, are driving worldwide workplace transformation.

Work is a concept that is both familiar and abstract to all of us. It is a place where we spend the majority of our life, something that gives, defines who we are, and requires output. But, rather than being a philosophical question, asking ourselves, "What is work, really?" could unlock an incredible amount of value.

What was work like in the past? What exactly is work these days? What does the future hold for work? Exploring these issues might help us better prepare for the changing nature of work.

Work was synonymous with craftsmanship, product development, and the delivery of complete outputs in the preindustrial economy. A tailor, for example, would take the customer's measurements and make the final adjustments in the finished set of suits. The craftsman is entirely responsible for the end-to-end process of delivering a product or outcome. The industrial revolution altered this view of work, as manufacturers discovered that by converting end-to-end processes into repeatable activities in which individuals (and, subsequently, machines) could specialize, things could be made faster and cheaper.

The concept of a "job" shifted from an integrated set of actions that generated a full product or conclusion to a collection of tasks that were not necessarily related to one another. With the advent of the rapid cognitive revolution, work has been redefined once again to generate beneficial human-machine collaborations, moving our notion of work from task fulfillment to problem-solving and human relationship management.

The way we divide tasks into jobs has already begun to shift as a result of technological advancements: robotics and robotic process automation, for example, have altered manufacturing and warehouses by boosting process efficiency and cutting costs, and digital reality technologies are enabling remote employees to overcome distance and task assignment limits. Over the previous thirty years, workforce demographics have shifted, with a workforce that is collectively older and more diverse.

The basic nature of the social contract between Leaders and employees has shifted significantly. Employers now have a wide range of options for recruiting workers, ranging from traditional full-time employees to managed services and outsourcing, independent contractors, gig workers, and crowdsourcing.

These emergent workforce types can help leaders solve problems, complete tasks, and develop more flexible and agile firms. Alternative employees are becoming more common; today, thirty-five percent of the US workforce is employed on a part-time, temporary project, or contract basis. This percentage is increasing as well; for example, the freelance workforce is rising at a higher rate than the whole workforce, with 8.1 percent of all employees now working as freelancers, compared to 2.6 percent of all employees.

The workplace changes as the "who" and "what" of work. Whereas in the past, physical proximity was essential for employees to get work done, the advent of digital communication, collaboration platforms, and virtual reality technology, as well as societal and commercial developments, have enabled and created the opportunity for more remote teams.

As they reinvent workplaces, companies can now arrange a variety of alternatives, from typical collocated offices to those that are remote and reliant on virtual connections

What We Were Used To

In offices across North America, the eight-to-five work schedule has ruled supreme for decades. Employees have regularly signed in at 8 AM and packed up for the day around 5 PM, regardless of their commute, schedule, or whether they consider themselves a "morning person." However, you may have recently noticed that some of your coworkers are arriving at work later in the day or leaving by mid-afternoon. You may have even seen that some folks don't come in at all, preferring to send emails well before 7 AM.

To put it another way, you may have seen the rise of flexible work arrangements and their impact on your team's performance. There are simply fewer reasons to come inside the office now that you can do most things remotely — whether it's hosting a conference through Zoom or taking care of operations online with payroll software. And it's not only your workplace that's changing. According to a recent poll conducted by The Conference Board of Canada, "almost nine out of ten (or 86 percent of) Canadian firms currently provide at least one form of flexible work option." While it's obvious that flexible working hours and telecommuting are in high demand, the reason for the move is a little more difficult. It's critical to understand why flexible work hours and telecommuting are swiftly becoming the norm, as well as what this implies for today's businesses, whether you're an employee or an employer.

You have to go back to Henry Ford and the American labor unions of the 1800s to understand the endurance of the eight-to-five. There was no limit to what employers might ask of employees at the time, therefore twelve-hour shifts (or more) were common. But something had to give, and the Ford Motor Company, thanks to worker riots and a lot of protesting, implemented a more acceptable five-day workweek with eight-hour workdays. The resulting surge in production and profit helped the model stay, and the eight-to-five has remained the norm in most of North America since then—until recently.

Workplaces have evolved considerably since Henry Ford's time, and the business landscape no longer resembles that of his time. It is no longer required for everyone to perform the same eight-hour shift due to the loss of manufacturing, the rise of women in the workplace, and, more recently, the acceleration of new technologies. Many alternatives have sprung up to address the changing demands of the modern workplace, with the nine-to-five increasingly becoming outmoded. Ad hoc remote days, flexible working hours, summer hours, job-sharing, full-time remote work, a compressed workweek, and even compressed days are examples of these options. Flexible work hours and telecommuting are by far the most common of these many options.

Employees can work outside of the usual eight-to-five, Monday-Friday work routine with flexible working hours. Employees, in other words, can tailor their timetables to meet their requirements. Starting work early and leaving early, starting later in the day and departing late, or even working on different days of the week are all possibilities.

Visual Approach to Management

In today's workplace, leadership entails a virtual approach to management and efficiency. The virtual office, in which employees work away from one another and management, is now a reality for many businesses, and all signs point to it becoming much more so in the future. Multi-site, multi-organizational, and dynamic virtual organizations. A virtual organization, at its most basic level, is a collection of enterprises, consultants, and contractors who have allied to leverage complementary capabilities in the pursuit of common strategic goals. The goals are frequently focused on a single project. This grouping, in and of itself, marks a significant shift in how we operate, and it offers two new issues for managers. Physical separation of workers and supervisors caused by information-age arrangements like telework and virtual teams is one of the issues. Many supervisors are now questioning themselves, "How can I manage them if I can't see them?" It identifies the virtual workplace's first managerial challenge: shifting from activity-based time management to project management (results-based).

The virtual workplace's second managerial problem is overcoming concerns about whether managers will still be appreciated by their employers if they supervise people who are not physically there. "What do I need you for?" a first-level manager recalls his boss said as he exited his office, looking around at the vacant cubicles. As we will explain in this post, fewer managers are not required.

Many businesses have used virtual workplaces and have seen the following advantages: Expenses on real estate have been reduced. By eliminating offices for all employees save those who genuinely need them, IBM saves forty to sixty percent per site annually. Northern Telecom believes that not having to keep an employee in a normal sixty-four-square-foot facility saves $2,000 per worker per year, excluding rant and annual running costs. Others anticipate a $2 return on investment for every $1 invested."

Productivity has increased. According to internal IBM studies, improvements of 15% to 40% are possible. The productivity of US West's teleworking staff increased by as much as 40%, according to the company. Profits are up. After transferring its salespeople to virtual office arrangements, Hewlett-Packard increased revenue per salesperson.

Lesson Learned:

The pandemic revealed several weaknesses in our leadership armor and caught many leaders by surprise as they incorrectly assumed they could continue leading by a *business-as-usual* approach. The most prevalent weakness being a leader's inability to manage productivity and performance without visual cues.

A Case Study: Leadership In The Pre-Covid-19 Era

Charles is the head of marketing in a local organization. He has been working in this firm for almost five years. Initially, he started his job here as an intern, but his hard work and focus have led him to promotions after promotions to where he is now. He became the head of the marketing department in 2018. This was two years before the outbreak of Covid-19. Over the years, he has proven to be a useful asset to the organization, and its sales have increased. The members of his team respect him, and they consider him a good and reliable leader. His efficient management skills have led to an increase in his team members' performance and, therefore, an increase in sales.

Charles has developed a good leadership strategy which he has used to take the organization to its current level. He has developed a good relationship with his employees. He always tells them the truth, especially on matters concerning the organization (Wilde, 2019). He ensures that he does not keep anything from them. Whenever any of his employees have an issue, problem or opinion, he makes time and listens to them. This makes the employees feel appreciated, and some of the opinions they give have been implemented and raised the organization's revenue. Charles always makes promises to his team members and ensures that he follows up on these promises (Wilde, 2019). He also promotes a positive work environment. It is through all these actions that Charles has earned the trust of his team members. Every year, since 2018, during the organization's awarding ceremony, Charles has been getting the "most trustworthy leader" award. The employees have put their trust in him, and they always nominate him for this award.

Charles has developed different leadership styles. He uses different styles depending on the situation at hand. In day-to-day tasks, he uses the participative leadership approach. He allows his team members to come up with most decisions concerning marketing (Cherry, 2020). He guides them and directs them into coming up with proper decisions. He also assigns them different tasks depending on their skills and capabilities. This has proven to be an effective long-term strategy. It allows the employees to develop their capabilities and improve their creativity and decision-making skills. Additionally, this strategy has helped to develop a positive working environment.

He also uses autocratic leadership skills. Whenever immediate decisions are needed, he uses his power as a leader to make this decision without necessarily involving his team members (Khan et al.). This decision is usually centralized, and the employees are expected to adhere to it. This one time, the organization's CEO requested the marketing department to come up with an investment strategy for the extra profits they had earned that year. Instead of Charles involving his team members in coming up with this decision, he made it himself. The employees agreed with him and supported his decision.

His most preferred style of leadership is the democratic leadership style. He holds departmental meetings weekly where the employees get to give their opinions. He gets to give feedback on the employees' performance and the progress of their various projects. Whenever they are coming up with a new product or a new marketing strategy, these meetings are increased to two meetings a week. The employees are given time to come up with ideas which they present during the departmental meetings. Charles then selects the most suitable and appropriate idea and brings it back to the departmental meetings. Together, they select the best marketing strategy or product to launch. This has positively impacted the employees since both their morale and productivity are increased (Cherry, 2020).

In the pre-covid-19 era, Charles and other leaders have used these different leadership styles to boost the employees' performance and to increase the organization's revenue.

SUGGESTIONS:

WHEN THIS HAPPENS…

When our company decides that a large population of our company will continue to work remotely on a flexible schedule…

RATHER THAN…

Relying on getting things done based on what *"I see being done…"*

AS a REIMAGINED LEADER, I WILL…

I will reset my own approach to planning, organizing, and checking to establish clear priorities, defined target dates, with plenty of conversation and opportunities to check progress along the way. I will evaluate my team based on output, deliverables, and results, not activity…

MYTH: People are in the office; they must be productive.

PART II

The Hybrid Leadership Tsunami

Chapter 2

The Global Pandemic: Everything Changed

The Bottom Line: The global pandemic changed not only where we work but also the way we work. People now expect more control over their work day and lives.

The industrialized world was seeing significant employment growth before the COVID crisis, to the point where The Economist magazine announced in May 2019 that "Most of the rich world is enjoying a jobs boom of unprecedented proportions" (The Economist 2019). Despite these optimistic trends, a cross-national Pew Research Center survey conducted in 2018 indicated that a majority of residents in advanced and emerging economies expected robots and computers to take over many occupations, worsening inequality and making it harder to obtain work (Wike and Stokes 2018). The COVID crisis has thrown these expectations out the window, bringing the United States' longest economic upswing to a stop and generating a worldwide increase in unemployment. Ironically, technological advancements in general, and automation in particular, played absolutely little role in this turn of events. Should we now turn our attention away from technology unemployment and toward more traditional threats? Or are all previous wagers void? The answer to both queries, in my opinion, is no. The present COVID crisis has made the trajectory of automation's impact on employment more visible, and what we're seeing gives us no reason to be complacent. Telepresence, urban de-densification, employment concentration in large enterprises, and general automation forcing all appear to be reshaping labor markets as a result of the COVID-19 pandemic. Although these reforms may improve efficiency, in the long run, they will intensify economic suffering for the least economically secure employees in our economy in the short and medium-term, notably those in the quickly developing but never-highly-paid personal services industry.

Employees Work-Life Balance before Covid-19

Although the term "work-life balance" was coined by the British in the 1980s, it is still relevant and hotly disputed today. The phrase has evolved over the decades, it was first coined by the Women's Liberation Movement to advocate for flexible work hours and maternity leave. Work-life balance has become a complex, genderless conundrum since the advent of the digital revolution, which spawned an "always culture."

Before we try to anticipate the future, let's take a look back at how we got here. Rapid technological developments and well-functioning institutions in the United States gave rising productivity and rapid, equally distributed wage gains to the great majority of employees in the decades immediately following World War II, from the mid-1940s to the late 1970s. From the mid-1970s until the present, this virtuous cycle has broken down. Even though aggregate productivity increased by almost seventy-five percent and average worker compensation increased by fifty percent between 1973 and 2016, the distribution of gains was so skewed that the median worker received less than a twenty percent rise in compensation. Yet, the distribution of gains was so skewed that the median worker received less than a twenty percent rise in compensation throughout these decades (Stansbury and Summers 2018). The disparity between increased productivity and stagnant median salaries over the previous four decades demonstrates that citizens have reason to be concerned about the effects of technology (in general) and automation (in particular) on worker and citizen welfare. New and emerging technologies will almost certainly increase overall economic production and societal affluence. However, the average person may not profit from these benefits. We wonder whether increased aggregate productivity leads to shared prosperity or merely increases inequality is highly dependent on the functioning of governance institutions, social investment, education, legislation, and other factors. We have argued earlier that the operation of governance institutions, social investment, education, law, and public and private leadership are critical in determining whether rising aggregate productivity translates into shared prosperity or merely rising inequality (Autor, Mindell, and Reynolds 2019).

Employees are dissatisfied despite significant visible progress at work. Getting a work-life balance was like scaling Mount Everest from sea level. Work-life balance entails examining how employees manage their time both at and away from work. Relationships, family duties, and other extra interests and hobbies may take up time outside of work. The ways a person uses to juggle all of their professional and personal obligations are referred to as work-life balance. The definition is straight forward but working professionals all around the world struggle to define it, let alone attain it. Those on the hunt are confronted with a complex terrain that includes thousands of articles, assertions, and claims about how to get there. With so many people feeling overwhelmed and unbalanced, it's important to reconsider how we think about work-life balance and how it will need to change for today's professionals.

It's the late stages of the Industrial Revolution and employees are overworked. The average worker in the United Kingdom works 14-16 hours each day, six days per week. These long hours had social and health consequences, especially for working parents with young children. This was brought to the attention of labor reformers until the United Kingdom agreed to reduce the number of hours worked by women and children.

Around the same period, the United States began recording its workers' hours and discovers that they work more than a hundred hours per week on average. The country's health and safety were jeopardized as a result of these long hours worked. After decades of worker protests, the United States changes the Fair Labor Standards Act and adopts the 40-hour workweek on October 24, 1940. This was the first step toward giving workers more time back.

Even though "work-life balance" was an invention in the 1980s in the United Kingdom as a pillar of the Women's Liberation Movement seeking to ensure Women's rights to flexible hours and maternity leave were championed by the movement. Working women were expected to work and maintain responsibilities for household and family rearing while males were socially unconstrained to pursue their career ambitions without bothering about housekeeping and family rearing. In the 1980s, a popular chant emphasized the clear work-life imbalance, posing the question of whether women in the office could truly "have it all." Despite sharing their concerns, women saw little alleviation or progress toward achieving work-life balance.

Today "work-life balance" has remained popular in recent years and has cut across the gender label to incorporate all employees' rights. This is partly due to the millennial generation's dominance in the workforce. Leaders have been putting in a lot of effort to figure out how to best appeal to millennial employees. With the millennial generation expected to account for seventy-five percent of the workforce by 2025, many business leaders believe it's time to rethink what work-life balance means.

A healthy work environment requires a good work-life balance. Maintaining a work-life balance reduces stress and helps to prevent job burnout. One of the most common health problems in the workplace is chronic stress. Hypertension, intestinal issues, chronic aches and pains, and cardiac difficulties are all possible side effects. Chronic stress has been related to an increased risk of depression, anxiety, and sleeplessness, which can have a severe influence on mental health.

Workplace burnout is caused by too much stress over a lengthy period. Employees who work a lot of overtime are at a higher risk of becoming burned out. Fatigue, mood fluctuations, impatience, and a drop in work performance are all symptoms of burnout. This is terrible news for companies, as the psychological and physical difficulties of burned-out employees cost an estimated $125 billion to $190 billion in healthcare expenses in the United States each year, according to Harvard Business Review.

Employers may save money and maintain a healthier, more productive workforce by developing a work environment that values work-life balance. But, exactly, what does work-life balance entail? That's where things start to get a little tricky. Work-life balance implies different things to different people. The knowledge and approach to work-life balance have evolved, and businesses may find it useful to identify the differences in opinions among Baby Boomers, Generation X, and Millennials.

Work-life balance has evolved to include both difficulties and initiatives aimed at helping employees manage their time effectively. Burnout prevention and stress management have also been added to the program. Today's employees seek better time management skills so they may spend more time with their families and pursue their hobbies. And, unlike in the 1980s, there is now a greater emphasis on gender-neutral work-life balance. Work-life balance should be attainable and distributed equally between men and women. (Source: EY's Global Generations Survey, 2015).

Even with these advancements, there is still a gap between employees' and human Resource (HR) professionals' perceptions of work-life balance. According to a Workplacetrends.com poll from February 2015, sixty-seven percent of HR professionals believe their employees are attaining work-life balance, whereas only forty-five percent of their employees believe the same.

Flexible schedules are atypical and popular options for organizations to assist employees to achieve work-life balance. Instead of working from 9 a.m. to 5 p.m., employees have the option to change their schedules. Work 10 a.m. to 6 p.m. or 7 a.m. to 3 p.m. with little planning or approval. There are, of course, drawbacks to this. Some contend that this strategy only moves time units without addressing a more fundamental need for quality time. Others have noted that, while flextime is appealing for recruitment, it might result in lower compensation, job stagnation, and even termination for younger workers.

Still, by blurring the barriers between work and life, digital integration jeopardizes the benefits of flextime. Employees frequently use their flextime to stay connected to work via the internet. It's becoming increasingly difficult to distinguish between job and life. It's even more difficult to draw a boundary between the two the more tech-savvy one is. Because technology and our "always on" lifestyle aren't going away anytime soon, the debate over work-life balance must adapt as well.

Many people wish to have children and raise them. Many others see that a job is required to assist support this family. The issue is that job and family duties sometimes tug workers in opposite ways. Remote work is one approach to assist alleviate this fight for work-life balance. Telecommuting became significantly more prevalent and accepted after the Internet and technology reached a certain degree of ubiquity and affordability. Working from home, for whatever reason, did not nearly attain its full potential before 2020. The coronavirus epidemic, on the other hand, maybe changing that. It became more critical than ever before with the compulsory shutdown of offices across the country in March 2020. The forced closing of offices across the country in March 2020 made it more necessary than ever for leaders to maintain a work-life balance. HR specialist Josh Bersin agrees, stating that one thing is certain: *the working landscape has changed, forever.*

Post Covid: Work-Life Blend

The line between home life and work life is becoming increasingly blurred as we navigate the raw and murky seas of COVID-19. Our lives, including how we manage our time, have changed tremendously, and we're now much more "turned on" than we were previously. With that in mind, how should employees deal with the new reality of work-life balance?

According to Dr. Melanie Peacock, associate professor of HR at Mount Royal University and recent winner of HRD Canada's Lifetime Achievement Award, noted that; *"Balancing work and life requirements will require attending to both physical and mental boundaries,"*

"Physical boundaries can best be set by allocating specific space at home for work activities. This helps to separate personal from professional time and provides cues to employees, and those they live with when the focus should be on work and as importantly when it should not.

"As important is the ability to turn one's thoughts away from work. It is too easy to be drawn back to a workspace, continuously think of work issues and check emails or texts on an ongoing basis. (Note, these were issues that needed to be addressed even before the changing landscape caused by COVID-19).

"Setting a work pattern, shutting the door (literally and figuratively) to a workspace, and training oneself to turn off work communication is critical. Asking friends and family to provide reminders to step away from work and learning to set, and then keep, personal commitments also helps to ensure that professional duties do not overwhelm one's time."

"As with any actions, employees need to set and practice patterns of behavior. By developing and honoring new routines which allow time for appropriate attention to both work and life requirements, a healthy balance can be maintained,"

Before the epidemic, a major argument for remote working was the fear that employees would become disengaged and productivity would suffer. However, new research reveals that working from home effectively means working more. Many employees in the United Kingdom, for example, are working an extra two hours every day. In the United States, it takes considerably longer.

The collapse of work-life boundaries, as well as the dread of being watched by employers, all appear to have contributed to people working harder for longer periods, according to a recent poll. Those who are combining job and caring responsibilities are frequently the most stressed. According to a recent UK poll, seventy-one percent of working women who requested vacation to care for their children were denied. The "sandwich generation," those responsible for childcare and elderly relatives, is also struggling.

All of these variables point to a future in which overworking is commonplace and the work-life balance becomes a pipe dream. This must not be allowed to continue.

Changing Attitudes About Working from Home

Around thirty-one percent of workers in the United States stated they had worked from home in the middle of March 2020, just before the coronavirus pandemic hit. However, just a few weeks later, in early April, that number had risen to sixty-two percent. It's safe to state that the coronavirus is causing an increase in the number of people who work from home. It wasn't always like this, though.

Even before we knew what the coronavirus was, some large corporations were restricting their employees' ability to work from home. It wasn't just the private sector that was cutting back on work-from-home benefits; several federal agencies were as well. It's easy to see why a growing number of businesses are encouraging employees to work from home. But, just a few years ago, why were they so reticent to enable employees to work from home? There are various theories to consider.

To begin with, some businesses believe it lowers employee productivity. When this is the case, it isn't always because the individual is working from home rather than from the office. Other factors could be at play, such as managers lacking the necessary skills to successfully oversee or monitor personnel from afar. Second, many bosses do not have faith in their staff. There are various reasons for this, including the idea that if "no one is looking," workers will slack off. Employers are concerned that employees working from home will be more likely to engage in inappropriate behavior, such as visiting inappropriate websites. Employees may mishandle corporate assets or information. Because of this mistrust, many firms attempt to monitor their workers who work from home. There's also the fundamental attribution error to consider. According to this idea, when people make judgments about others, they place a larger focus on the person's personality attributes and less on the person's situation. As a result, when someone works from home, the basic attribution problem might be exacerbated.

If an office worker isn't at their desk, for example, a manager may believe they're at a meeting or using the restroom. If the same thing happens with a remote worker, the manager might presume the employee is watching TV or conducting errands. Fourth, many companies believe it is necessary to spend time with coworkers or otherwise have "face time." This form of in-person engagement is said to boost morale, workplace harmony, and productivity. Despite employer fears, working from home appears to be becoming the new normal for some employees. This is due to several benefits that come with remote work.

The Advantages of Telecommuting

Though (most) workplaces are not blatantly hostile to human life, they are costly, redundant locations for executing activities that many employees might tele present from elsewhere, although at the expense of the vital social components of work that they permit. Employers incur significant indirect costs not only in building and maintaining physical workplaces but also in the necessity for employees to be physically present in offices. According to the Census Bureau, Americans spend an average of twenty-seven minutes commuting to work each way, accumulating to two hundred and twenty-five hours a year (U.S. Census Bureau 2019; authors' calculations). Many of us who do "knowledge work" may have been so accustomed to "being there" that we failed to recognize the quick gains in the next best option: not being there.

Long after the COVID crisis has passed, it appears almost inevitable that the percentage of workers who work partially or entirely from home will be significantly higher than it was before the crisis. Indeed, after the pandemic has gone, employers in the United States predict that the number of working days delivered from home will triple (Altig et al. 2020). Of course, this projection only applies to the top quartile of higher-educated professionals whose work can be done remotely (Dingel and Neiman 2020), and we'll go through the consequences for other workers later. These same concerns almost certainly apply to business travel: much of this physical travel was formerly necessary, but telepresence has made it much less so, and companies will need to reevaluate how much of it is still worth paying for. The crisis has also accelerated the adoption of telemedicine for the "hands-off" delivery of a subset of medical services (Hollander and Carr 2020). In the near term, telemedicine has made social separation easier. In the long term, it will save both clinicians and patients time in the office.

Remote work may usually be divided into three categories: enhanced employee morale, increased productivity, and cost savings. The most significant benefit of remote work may be improved employee morale. This could be due to a variety of variables, one of the most essential of which is a better work-life balance. In a recent FlexJobs survey of more than four thousand respondents working from home in response to the coronavirus, seventy-three percent reported that working from home helped them achieve a better work-life balance. They were able to spend more time with their partner, family, or pets as a result of this.

A better work-life balance has other advantages. Women who were allowed to work from home rather than returning to the office after giving birth had reduced levels of depression, according to a 2015 study. Employees are also less concerned about taking time off to care for a child, spouse, or another family member. If the employee is already at home, they may be less concerned about upsetting the boss by taking a few hours off to spend time with a youngster. It may also lessen the likelihood of prejudice towards caregivers. Working from home can enhance employee productivity by as much as 25%. According to the FlexJobs survey, 51% of respondents thought working from home made them more productive. Only 5% thought they were less productive. Fewer interruptions, working in a more comfortable environment, and not having to worry about workplace drama were all factors that contributed to increased productivity. However, there is more time to do tasks. In the FlexJobs poll, for example, more than a third of respondents spent two or more hours each workday commuting to and from the office.

Finally, the employer benefits from cost savings. An on-site worker, for example, costs a business $10,000 per year in real estate expenditures. Business Leaders may be able to save money on compensation as a result of this. According to an Owl Labs survey from 2020, twenty-three percent of full-time employees are willing to take a wage drop of more than ten percent to work from home at least part of the time.

Then there's the simplicity with which businesses can hire new employees. This could be attributed to factors such as geography, where being in the workplace is less important, and attracting millennial and Generation X workers. In addition to recruiting, there may be a boost in employee loyalty. According to the FlexJob poll, 81 percent of respondents felt that having remote work opportunities would boost their loyalty to their employer.

As more individuals are vaccinated against Covid-19 and the world returns to some kind of routine, many organizations are soliciting opinions from employees on how, when, and even if to return to work following the outbreak. While the transition to remote work was one of the most significant effects of Covid-19 on the workplace, ushering in changes in operations and mindsets that would outlast the pandemic, the past year has highlighted and given rise to concerns that go far beyond work modes.

Many employees' feelings of well-being suffered during the pandemic as a result of unprecedented levels of stress, anxiety, uncertainty, and social isolation, leading companies to consider various approaches to assist the physical and mental well-being of their workforces.

Many companies have been collecting the viewpoints of office workers across the United Kingdom since the outbreak began, to better understand their genuine needs and goals as organizations strive to chart a route forward. A creator of a lifestyle insurance firm believes that the discovery that gathering such information can help avoid wasting money on employee engagement programs that aren't based on a detailed understanding of employees' attitudes and requirements.

One of the most important findings from a poll is that employees are increasingly expecting their employers to do more to improve their overall quality of life. In light of the findings, here are some suggestions for business leaders: Encourage employees to take breaks, create a supportive workplace atmosphere, and conduct regular check-ins and surveys on employee well-being.

Developing the Complete Workforce's Skill Set

For most Companies, traditionally, talent acquisition was confined to a few virtual workers, with the majority of their personnel based in pre-determined geographic regions. Now, a big percentage of workers will continue to work from home or in a "hybrid" environment, creating new markets for talent acquisition.

Enterprises have been changing their employee development strategies even before the outbreak. Accelerated job automation, rapid AI adoption, analytics integration into business processes, and the rise of remote work are just a few of the technology-driven trends that are changing the nature of work and the skills that will be required in the not-too-distant future.

Workplace restructuring has far-reaching ramifications for workforce development. According to the World Economic Forum's (WEF) Future of Jobs Report 2020, a shift in the division of labor between humans and computers might disrupt eighty-five million jobs by 2025. While this is alarming, the research also predicts that ninety-seven million new employment will be created to accommodate the new human-machine work division.

Continuous reskilling and upskilling are required for an expanding spectrum of company functions, as new roles are created while others become superfluous. According to the World Economic Forum (WEF) report, employers expect that roughly forty percent of their staff would need to be reskilled in six months or less, and ninety-four percent of business executives believe people will learn these new skills on the job, up from sixty-five percent in 2018. Talent acquisition, on the other hand, used to be confined to a few virtual workers, with the majority of their staff based in pre-determined geographic regions. That is undoubtedly changing now, as a result of the pandemic, substantial percentages of workers will continue to work remotely or in a "hybrid" setting, hence creating new markets for talent acquisition. Consider a situation in which your company's employees are forced to adjust their work habits almost immediately as a result of a catastrophe. Despite your initial concerns that the strain would be too much, you find that this new method of working could be a long-term blueprint. That is what many CEOs around the world are discovering as they respond to the COVID-19 crisis.

Consider the experience of a pharmaceutical corporation with over ten thousand sales representatives. It transitioned from an offline to a hundred percent remote-working paradigm in February. As the containment phase draws to a close, you may expect remote working to fade as well. However, the company now intends to adopt a permanent 30-percent-online–70-percent-offline working paradigm, allowing it to capitalize on its sales agents' newly earned talents.

Even before the current crisis, new technologies and ways of working were causing disruptions in employment and the skills required to do them. Because of automation and artificial intelligence, the McKinsey Global Institute estimated in 2017 that three hundred and seventy-five million employees, or fourteen percent of the global workforce, will have to change occupations or learn new skills by 2030. According to a recent McKinsey Global Survey, eighty-seven percent of executives are experiencing or expecting skill gaps in the workforce within the next several years. However, less than half of those polled had a clear idea of how to solve the situation.

The coronavirus pandemic has heightened the urgency of this subject. Individuals in all industries must learn to adapt to quickly changing circumstances, and businesses must learn how to match those workers to new roles and activities. This dynamic encompasses more than remote working or the role of automation and artificial intelligence. It's about how leaders may reskill and upskill their employees in the post-pandemic environment to deliver new business models.

Companies should design a talent strategy that improves employees' vital digital and cognitive talents, as well as their social and emotional skills, adaptability, and resilience, to face this challenge. Now is the time for businesses to commit to reskilling by increasing their learning spending. Companies will be better prepared for future upheavals if they develop this muscle.

Before the crisis, remote working was becoming more popular, but the pandemic has proven that telecommuting is here to stay. According to a recent Gartner CFO survey, over three-quarters of CFOs aim to "shift at least five percent of previously on-site staff to permanently remote employment post-COVID-19." Although many employees "learned by doing" or obtained "quick and dirty" training during the first phase of the crisis, prolonged remote working will almost certainly pose an upskilling problem. Salespeople, for example, will have to change their focus from setting up video meetings to effectively managing client connections in remote locations.

A Review of Investment for Companies

Recreational Equipment Incorporated (REI) put its newly constructed corporate headquarters in Bellevue, Washington, up for sale in August before ever moving into the building.

It was a spectacular 180-degree turn. When REI revealed its intentions for the campus in 2016, it stated that it would establish a gathering area that would stimulate innovation and bring thousands of employees together. The outdoor recreation store chose to sell the 8-acre compound because many of its staff were working remotely due to the epidemic. It soon shifted its office space ambitions to include smaller, satellite locations all across the Seattle suburbs. By September, the Bellevue building had been sold to Facebook. REI also opened its first satellite office in Issaquah, Washington, in February, a nearly 70,000-square-structure that can accommodate up to 400 people and is surrounded by hiking trails, lakes, and parks. The firm is also experimenting with a concept that permits staff to work from home up to five days per week.

REI's executive vice president of technology and operations, Chris Putur, said, "We want to establish a workplace that is incredibly adaptable for our staff." "In 2020, we were astounded by how nimble, innovative, and productive the team could be." REI's blueprint for its future workplace is only one example of the commercial office market's ongoing transformation.

Just like REI, many Companies used to invest in fixed assets, such as buildings, offices, and infrastructure; now, that model has been altered as a result of the pandemic, with fewer investments and demand for big, well-organized spaces that were once considered "cubical farms." Business leaders find the reality tuned in their favor as they can cut costs immensely. The success of several industries in operating remotely has been one of the most remarkable characteristics of the overall operating environment in 2020. While not perfect, the near-universal use of virtual meeting software and services has offered clear evidence that many American employees can perform well outside of the traditional office setting. As a result, entire businesses where location is not critical to success are already evaluating their future physical footprint requirements to uncover potential occupancy cost savings. Companies will more likely save money by shifting to smaller premises or subleasing portions of their current physical footprint. While reducing occupancy costs by considerable percentages on an anticipated P&L is the aim and appears to be a good idea, it will take time and money for businesses to free themselves from long-term mortgages and leases.

Workers in the United States have faced several logistical and even behavioral issues as a result of work-from-home instructions. While working remotely has several drawbacks, the current operational environment has created numerous examples of cost savings. Giving people a laptop isn't the only benefit of remote working. Some aspects of office life can't be duplicated. However, old work conventions are vital, such as the belief that once you leave the office, your workday is over. "It's not so much working from home as it is sleeping at the office," one CEO explained.

Companies must assist their employees in establishing those limits for working from home to be sustainable: the type of interaction that used to take place in the hallway may be handled with a fast phone call rather than a videoconference. Setting "office hours" for specific groups, sharing time-tracking methods, and announcing that emails will not be addressed after a certain hour may also be beneficial.

Not every business can be a beacon of hope. However, every company can develop a plan that outlines what needs to be done (and by whom) to achieve a stated goal, ensure the resources necessary to achieve that goal, train personnel in digital technologies and cybersecurity, and bring leadership to bear. To get out of "pilot purgatory," as most digital-transformation programs did before the COVID-19 disaster, it means focusing on outcomes (not favored technology), learning through experience, and developing an ecosystem of tech suppliers, rather than doing the same thing the same way.

Globally, businesses have quickly responded to the pandemic. There's been a lot less handwringing and a lot more focusing on the task at hand. Stop for those who believe and hope that everything will return to normal. They aren't going to. Accepting the reality that the future isn't what it used to be and thinking about how to make it work is preferable.

When things are tough, hope and optimism can take a beating. To hasten the recovery, leaders must inspire a sense of purpose and hope, as well as make the case that even the most uncertain future can be made better with effort.

PART III

Surviving the Shock Wave & Wake

Chapter 3

Challenges the New Normal Creates for Leaders

The Bottom Line: The COVID-19 global pandemic exposed hybrid work challenges centered around the reinvented workplace and workforce.

There's No Turning Back Now

2020 was a year of uncertainty, but there is one thing we know for sure coming out of it: remote work is here to stay long after the global pandemic ends.

In an August 2020 survey taken by Software Advice, 49% of HR leaders plan to hire more fully remote workers when the pandemic ends. The same respondents also note that their companies plan to allow 46% of their existing workers to work remotely more often. In another survey just two months earlier, 56% of employees told Software Advice they would prefer to work from home more often when the pandemic ends, and an additional 17% stating they'd prefer working from home permanently.

Employees had anticipated flexible work options as a tool to boost motivation and promote work/life balance well before the outbreak. With the outbreak of the pandemic, it has become increasingly evident that flexibility is also essential for keeping workers safe.

Working from home has become the norm, and we've progressed from digitizing the relationship between a company and its customers to digitizing the relationship between an employer and an employee. This reality underlies the global response to COVID-19, which has resulted in the workplace's most rapid transition. We've been propelled forward, catching up with trends like automation, digitization, and innovation.

Companies are at a crossroad: those who seize post-COVID chances will be in a better position to retain and attract talents once the environment stabilizes. Those that refuse to change, on the other hand, will be left behind, exposing their workforce to higher financial risks, including layoffs and closures.

Before the crisis, remote working was becoming more popular, but the pandemic has proven that telecommuting is inevitable. Leaders must learn how to lead their teams digitally while building social capital and maintaining cohesion without the benefit of informal coffee, lunch, or corridor discussions. As businesses consider returning to work, a new set of skills is likely to emerge to help with the transition.

Regardless, the new normal has placed enormous pressure on corporate leaders and executives. It's easy to be a good leader when things are going well for the company and the economy, but it's an entirely different task when things aren't going so well or when there's the possibility of a permanent staff change. Leaders who once flourished within the confines of a traditional, physical workplace are now forced to navigate the uncharted realm of leading large populations of workers remotely and online for extended periods of time, if not indefinitely.

These obvious shifts present significant difficulties for leaders and how they respond to them. As a result, we'll focus on the four main challenges that the new normal presents to leaders - these include: *blended life balance, performance management, communication,* and *culture.*

This means as a leader in an organization, if you fail to adapt, you'll risk lower productivity and engagement, and possibly even worse, higher levels of employee turnover.

Four Core Challenges for Leaders

Challenge #1: Culture Challenges - Connecting

Losing the company's identity, its very soul, is the greatest challenge leaders face as they adapt to the life in the new normal of hybrid work. The organization culture is the very lifeblood that connect its values with intangible sets of behaviors by its people – *"It defines how a workforce operates and interacts with one another."*

In a survey by Nulab, 83% of people said that they weigh company culture when choosing an employer and 90% said that "company culture" is important toward being productive. The disconnect leaders must contend with is prevalent because two-thirds of U.S. employees told Software Advice they felt more connected to their company's culture while working in the office compared to working from home. Only a meager 13% felt more connected while working from home.

Many firms' capacity to adjust to large-scale telework and other changes necessitated by the pandemic could be attributed to seasoned, mature leadership teams that already knew each other. The question is whether, under the new normal, we will have the atmosphere that fosters the kind of relationships and commitment that promotes an organization's long-term health. Is it possible to build and foster great leadership teams in an increasingly atomized society with a less physical presence and shared experience?

During the pandemic, everyone is suffering. The engine is a term used to describe the job of the leader. They, like everyone else in an organization, are dealing with a variety of personal issues while attempting to balance them with the demands of the workplace. However, leaders (executives, managers, and supervisors) are fundamentally responsible for other employees and are in charge of setting the tone of the organization, enforcing the culture and rules, a plethora of workplace administrative duties, achieving organizational goals, and being in the position of trying to make it all work in a highly dynamic environment. Leadership will have to deal with the injustices and jealousies that may arise as a result of this. Leaders have a lot to sort out, from work hours to work locations to virtual personnel engaging with those who want to be in the office. How can leaders stay sane in the face of so much pressure?

The challenge for leaders is to lead intelligently, purposefully, and effectively during a period of new normalcy. How can we seek clarity to help us survive—and possibly thrive—during this vital period, when so much has changed in the way leaders manage teams, deal with issues, and prioritize?

Employees are also dealing with more than just learning new technology or adjusting to working from home; they are working full-time while coping with a worldwide health catastrophe and attempting to change their entire working style to fit the new reality. Remote management puts strain on the organization's culture, including a new expectation for leaders to educate and empower their people to perform at their best amid a period of greater stress—all from the comfort of their own homes.

However, as we move toward more permanent remote workforces, leaders will face additional challenges, such as how to retain people engaged who have never met in person. How can we continue to provide virtual instruction and deliveries of all types in a fast-developing virtual environment while keeping our attention? And, more importantly, how can we anticipate the issues that tomorrow's virtual world will provide and act to prevent the future risk?

Also, Leadership is likewise concerned with how a company keeps its identity in the new normal, the hybrid redesigned workplace. How will organizations keep their "personality," their cultures, with upwards of thirty to sixty percent of people not returning? When up to sixty percent of employees aren't in the office at the same time on any given day, it's difficult for them to feel connected. Due to the previously mentioned blended life synchronization difficulty, even members of the same team may be dispersed throughout the day, working at different times and utilizing different media - all at the same time. How does a business "maintain its soul"? Leaders must do it on a micro-level for their teams and small groups, and senior leaders have identified ways to accomplish it at the macro-organizational enterprise level. How will leaders, both on the front lines and across the business, monitor the pulse of their teams and workforce in the freshly rebuilt workplace? What will be the telltale signals that the culture is unhealthy or stagnant?

Culture is the glue that holds organizations together and allows them to operate and thrive. It is made up of shared stories, experiences, and behavioral norms. Most people, for example, would not come up to a face-to-face meeting with their faces hidden. However, with the rapid shift to remote work, something that was never a concern previously is now being debated. It could be deemed impolite by certain people. It makes no difference to others. What are the consequences of not having a standard for using available video to view someone's face? Is this an issue that needs to be addressed to foster a positive culture?

Physically demanding workplaces create pressures that give rise to a slew of new conventions. This creates voids that, if not filled, can lead to poisonous, organization-killing cultures. In a more physically oriented environment, things like working hours, forming informal relationships based on local events, commuting, and simply "seeing" one other came naturally. To survive in the new normal, leaders will need to pay close attention to building and modifying their culture. What is a leader's role?

Challenge #2: Blended Life Balance Challenges – Employee Burnout

A respondent in a recent survey shared her experience as saying: "My youngest son just popped out through the camera making some hilarious face one time when I was in a virtual meeting with other coworkers. Even though I ran him away and slammed the door behind him, I felt awkward and quickly apologized. Situations like this are a harsh reality that comes with having a blended life balance. As difficult as it may be for some, we can no longer divide our professional and personal lives. The equilibrium is showing who we are in our most natural state." Life and work are more intertwined than ever before in people's DNA. This isn't the same thing as "virtual labor" as we once knew it. The long-awaited flexibility is no longer limited to a few people, either as fulfill-time off or offshore employees; it is already a reality for a large number of people, with the pandemic contributing to a sixty percent increase in the number of remote workers. It used to be a few virtual employees who worked from home in companies with some offshore staff working in other time zones, primarily in information technology (IT). Now, however, multiple people in every department, from Human Resources to Finance, are on different work schedules to allow more personal and life flexibility.

According to a new study, working from home is not proving to be the dream experience that many employees had hoped for. They believe that working from home while wearing pajamas has become a reality. Longer hours, more virtual meetings, and blurring barriers between business and home life are common trade-offs. Some people benefit and like working from home, but experts conclude that working remotely takes its toll on the majority of people.

According to various research, people who work from home work longer hours. Personal activities and job activities appear to be more confused when people are not in an office atmosphere, based on my experience and talks with many people. At the same time, people who work from home no longer must commute. Lunch breaks might be more efficient time.

One of the most common fears about allowing workers to work from home is that their productivity will be at the receiving end. Images of employees working from home abound, with parents attempting to work while babysitting, folks conversing on a Zoom meeting in their jammies, and others raiding the refrigerator among them. Nicholas Bloom, a Stanford economist, investigated the impact of a Chinese travel agency on productivity and discovered positive results. Working from home required, however, that they have an area designated as an "office" in which to function and that no young children were present during the day. When Bloom started working from home and had four young children, he concluded that widespread working from home could lead to a global productivity dip, which would slow economic growth for years. Although Bloom's survey was more concerned with the impact of working from home on productivity, the reality is that many people are now sharing more details about their personal lives and activities with coworkers.

An integrated work-life means that people are now sharing their "true selves" with their coworkers and bosses, without a doubt. There was a "Professional Persona" before the pandemic - how people behaved, worked, and what they chose to communicate with colleagues - but now there is the "Real Self," which is transparent, human, simple, and as frail as the feeble persona. Employees are lowering their defenses, revealing themselves in real life, dealing with real personal difficulties that can spill over into their work lives. There was a time when a woman hopping around on camera trying to hide her tiny child who was trying to get into the video picture wasn't accepted; now, post-COVID, it's not only accepted, but a commonplace, and it's real life. We frequently see pets on screens, as well as individuals eating sandwiches while participating in virtual meetings.

Leaders also confront the problem of successfully coordinating their team so that they may remain professional even when they are at home. Often, the most common issues range from how do leaders encourage employees they don't see very frequently to how do they motivate people they don't see very often to maintain productivity? When the employees are dispersed across numerous sites, how can they stay productive, efficient, and effective? How can we keep our employees motivated and engaged? How do we ensure that employees' well-being is protected when they work from home? How are we going to be able to be everywhere we're needed?

Once, you could look up and observe an ocean of busy people getting work done, how then can we know that everyone on our team is 'pulling their weight,' providing what we need, and managing their workload? After all, one of the main worries that Senior Executives have about flexible or remote work is whether or not work will get done!

Challenge #3: Performance Management Challenges – Giving Feedback

Do you know how much and how quickly your remote workforce completes tasks? The answers to these questions are ambiguous for many leaders. When working remotely and not knowing their productivity, it's difficult to tell if someone is underutilized or not contributing their fair share.

Many leaders have accepted the new normal because of the uncertainty posed by Covid-19 and have accepted remote work or hybrid work as the norm. While over a quarter of the US workforce already works from home at least part of the time, the new restrictions will require many employees — and their supervisors — to work out of the office for the first time, separating them from one another.

Although it is generally better to set clear remote-work policies and training in advance, this level of preparation may not be possible in times of crisis or other rapidly changing conditions. As a result, one of the primary issues that leaders confront in this scenario is how to boost remote employees' engagement and productivity without putting in a lot of effort or pressure.

Leaders were concerned that high-performing employees would suffer losses in job performance and engagement if they began working remotely without enough preparation and training because they didn't grasp the characteristics that can make remote work particularly hard.

Managers and their staff are equally concerned about the lack of face-to-face supervision. They frequently voice their dissatisfaction with the lack of face-to-face interaction. Supervisors are concerned that their staff will not work as hard or as efficiently as they should (though research indicates otherwise, at least for some types of jobs). On the other side, many employees struggle with a lack of managerial assistance and communication. Employees may believe that their remote bosses are out of touch with their requirements and, as a result, are neither supportive nor helpful in completing their tasks.

Hence, remote leaders must devise methods for tracking all employees' productivity. Setting up metrics for how much work should be performed each day, such as creating and maintaining a company blog, scheduling twenty social media posts per hour, making one hundred and fifty cold calls per shift, and increasing virtual meetings, are all examples of this.

In many cases, leaders' attempts to address the lack of visual clues and opportunities with complete teams of individuals working from home to "see" people working at their desks have resulted in the creation of more meetings by default, which is a source of concern on both sides. Virtual meetings are held utilizing software such as ZOOM, MS Teams, GoToMeeting, and others. Without a doubt, executives use meetings as a crutch to compensate for not being able to see their employees in person, so they rely on video and audio. Overload challenges were met as a result of the outcomes. Most leaders have never or just sometimes had the opportunity to manage a remote worker, let alone a team of remote workers. Leaders will struggle to provide coaching, feedback, create employee relationships, and measure performance as more individuals stay at home or work from home in a hybrid approach after COVID.

Due to the varied time zones, one of the most difficult aspects of working remotely for global teams is organizing a phone conference or a video meeting. This is exacerbated by independent contractors with erratic work schedules. Knowing where your participants reside and their regular schedules can help you find a time that works for everyone.

Leaders must be willing to refrain from forcing meetings on their remote employees and instead seek out online solutions to assist in the scheduling of calls, video conferences, and meetings with distant teams. Some methods make the process of organizing a meeting less stressful, from a basic online poll that displays selected days and times that team members can choose to calendaring apps and a range of websites and free hosts that analyze participant availability. (It also helps if team members have flexible schedules, as some time zones don't align well with regular working hours.)

Employees and independent contractors should be compensated for participating in virtual team calls and meetings. Some project managers expect project-based freelancers to take calls for free or as part of a fixed cost for working on a project, even though they wouldn't attend a work-related meeting off the clock. When freelancers and contractors aren't accessible for calls or meetings, these managers are frequently surprised. If a meeting or phone call is required and work-related, consider compensating employees to attend.

Challenge #4: Communication Challenges - Collaboration

When working with remote teams, communication is crucial to success. It's important to get everyone's feedback and to know what each person is working on. It's not always simple to foster open communication when teams operate remotely. Email marketing is typically perceived as a formal technique that does not allow for rapid conversations.

Collaboration and communication have been rated as a top difficulty by remote employees in Buffer's annual State of Remote Work poll for the past three years, and it's easy to see why. Operating at different places (and even different time zones) is a poor substitute for gathering in a room to discuss ideas and make decisions, as any manager will easily admit.

At the very least, technology can assist in bridging the communication gap between remote personnel. There are four sorts of communication tools available to on-site employees that require a software counterpart for remote employees to be as effective:

The meeting room: You'll need software that allows you to gather your remote staff in one (virtual) location for face-to-face meetings. This is possible with the correct video conferencing software.

The blackboard: It's extremely tough to share and track ideas through the internet. To assist your remote staff with their brainstorming needs, look into whiteboard software or document management software.

The Task list: You'll need software to assign work responsibilities and keep everyone updated on the status of major projects. For this purpose, task management software or project management software may be appropriate.

The water cooler: Workers (even those who work from home) require a space to chat casually. We recommend collaboration software for those fast exchanges because you won't be able to walk by someone's workstation or run into them in the hallways.

Meetings are not only inconvenient because, even as technology catches up to the enterprise, large-scale adoption and use by companies to support high volumes of traffic, users of various tech skill levels, experience, age, and proficiency still struggle to replicate the simplicity and ease of walking into a room together. Furthermore, internet meetings might obscure the importance of human bodily cues and body language in our conversation. To exacerbate the problem, workers can "hide" and mute in meetings, stay off-camera, and only partially interact or participate, reducing cooperation effectiveness and resulting in communication issues.

Many remote teams circumvent this by establishing a specialized communication space, whether for workers in the same department or freelancers working on the same project. Slack, an internal team communication application allows for communication over several channels. Employees in the future will be able to see the answers to frequently asked questions. Remote workers won't feel separated from one another no matter what tool they use, as long as there's a mechanism to support two-way conversation.

Six Foundations of the Reimagined Workplace & Workforce

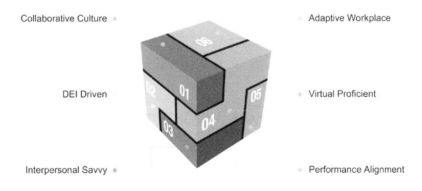

The pandemic has compelled the development of new working methods. Organizations must rethink their work and the role of offices in ensuring that people have safe, productive, and pleasurable workplaces and lifestyles. Many businesses around the world have risen to the challenge, responding quickly to protect employees and transition to a new way of working that even the most comprehensive business continuity plans had not anticipated. Leaders from a variety of industries will apply the lessons learned from this large-scale work-from-home experiment to reimagine how work is done—and what role offices should play—in new and innovative ways. Leaders must be proactive in implementing these six foundations of the reinvented workforce and workplace to be productive and overcome the obstacles that the new normal has brought us.

Foundation #1: Collaborative Culture

The workplace of a corporation reveals a lot about its corporate culture. The physical workplace is a company's greatest tool for helping employees feel engaged, valued, and empowered to take ownership of their work-related tasks. It is an outward expression of the firm's values, beliefs, traditions, attitudes, and so much more. Employees feel more connected to their companies and anchored in the purpose they bring to the company's mission after spending time in this environment. As a result of the typical office operations pattern, executives have found strategies to encourage collaboration and teamwork.

Leaders must now, more than ever, rethink collaborative culture in the new normal. The hybrid workplace has revolutionized the way employees work independently and in "pods" (ad hoc teams), as well as collaborate with other teams or functions. With everyone working split schedules, some days in the office, some days remote, and other days from alternate locations outside the home, such as the park, their children's school, and so on, the collaborative dynamic has shifted dramatically. As a result, collaboration in the hybrid workplace becomes "untethered" in terms of location, physical space, media (laptop vs. iPad vs. smartphone), and time. Employees may occasionally feel isolated or left out as a result of this over time.

According to a recent study conducted by We Work, working from home has resulted in a 15% reduction in employees' ability to meet and brainstorm. That may not seem like a significant reduction, but there are only two outcomes if we get more done while collaborating less. One is that our work isn't as precise as it used to be. The other is that it lacks the inventiveness required for a successful and long-term outcome.

Every team, whether it has two or two hundred members, requires the ability to cooperate, share, and learn on multiple levels. We become further away from recognizing the significance of these encounters the longer we avoid face-to-face interactions. When everyone is huddled around their computer, it's impossible to achieve the same degree of creativity and communication.

Furthermore, when employees have less personal interactions with their coworkers and supervisors, our ability to retain them plummets.

Some of these individualized experiences will organically resurface over time. However, for employees who will continue to work from home or for hybrid work teams, it will be critical to establishing a collaborative and interactive atmosphere. We need to build a hybrid collaboration, which includes informal interaction, one-on-one interaction within the team, scheduled face-to-face, leaders' one-on-one check-ins, and offsite in-person meetings regularly.

Foundation #2 DEI Driven

In the workplace, diversity, equality, and inclusion (DEI) is critical. It is now more important than ever to apply interdisciplinary thinking to turn discourse into action. However, improving structural and social constraints and achieving a stimulating and humane working environment requires awareness, sensitivity, and teamwork.

"Research has shown that diverse groups are more effective at problem-solving than homogeneous groups, and policies that promote diversity and inclusion will enhance our ability to draw from the broadest possible pool of talent, solve our toughest challenges, maximize employee engagement and innovation, and lead by example by setting a high standard for providing access to opportunity to all segments of our society."1 — Barack Obama

Making DEI a strategic imperative may help your company gain real financial value, recruit top personnel, and produce innovative results. As a result, at the heart of the rebuilt company, workplace, and workforce, a new hybrid leader is the vital advancement of inclusion and diversity fused into today's organization's DNA. Implicit bias must be addressed due to increased social, morale, and awareness.

Foundation #3 Interpersonal Savvy

1st of July, 2020 COVID-19, we all know, transformed the way we live and work in an instant. What we don't know is how the health and economic crises will unfold, as well as what attitude shifts will occur.

However, one thing is certain: to succeed in the redesigned workplace, businesses will need to develop their employees' digital, cognitive, social, and emotional, as well as adaptation and resilience skills. Leaders aren't the only ones who need to improve their soft skills. Employees in these reimagined businesses must have a high level of self-awareness and emotional intelligence. The ability to connect and communicate more effectively in the digital realm necessitates it. In-depth reflection and applied social skills, using tools such as the Enneagram 9 Type Descriptors to dig below the surface of personality types and traits to learn more about what they and their coworkers fear and are motivated by. Otherwise, the collaboration component will be devoid of the vital fuel that people and teams require.

Foundation #4 Virtual Proficient

Most businesses must reskill their more seasoned staff to adapt to the megabyte speed of social platforms to keep workers in step with the economy and the millennium workforce, who live and flourish on platforms like Twitter, Snapchat... Companies have a generational divide that has been exacerbated by COVID... Poor virtual meeting experiences, difficulties with chat, and ineffective usage of digital team collaboration platforms such as MS Teams, ZOOM, and GotoMeeting, to name a few, were among the symptoms. Companies must consider technology and infrastructure limitations in addition to skills – increased bandwidth for the organization to accommodate a litany of constant remote meetings, ways to work within their communities to upgrade Internet delivery in the communities where their workforce resides to maximize remote efficiency, and in some cases, simply enable it. Then there's the matter of dealing with cyber-threats and ensuring data security. Virtual expertise encompasses more than just the technology, infrastructure, and support systems. It's having a business of cybersecurity specialists on every digital platform it operates and supports, which goes beyond user application proficiency. User-level phishing or threat penetration, rather than server-direct attacks, are the most common sources of digital dangers.

Foundation #5 Performance Alignment

It's been argued for a long time that remote work is the way of the future. Remote work has now become a reality for hundreds of millions of employees as a result of the global pandemic's consequences, as well as the progressive trend towards a remote-first society.

Despite the tremendous benefits of remote work, it also presents a distinct set of problems. Remote work has forced the need for employers and managers to track performance in remote teams, in addition to challenges such as hiring remote workers, security, communication, and project management. However, keeping track of projects and specific tasks, as well as overall performance, can be tough.

Companies must emphasize the benefits of a flexible working environment to sustain team cohesion and ensure that team members feel included. You don't want a haphazard and disjointed remote work policy, where certain team members are required to work in the office every day while others are semi- or remote. This will just add to the tense atmosphere at your office.

With employees working on sporadic schedules, CEOs and leaders must synchronize activities and priorities for their teams to meet specific needs and deadlines while maintaining flexibility and inclusiveness.

"Creating a structure and architecture for decision-making and good communication is key," writes Raphael Bick in a McKinsey essay. Remember this when stating what you want, how you want it delivered, and when you want it done: The clearer your explanations are, the better. The easier it will be for remote employees to meet their job needs if clear expectations are established from the start. As a result, you won't need to monitor remote team performance as closely.

Foundation #6 Adaptive Workplace

The typical "office day" has evolved. Adaptive workplaces, a more fluid model that gives employees more flexibility to work from wherever they are most productive, allowing them to do their best job, and producing better results for employers, will likely be the way of the future.

The physical aspect of the office is part of the adaptive workplace. Companies will need to rethink office arrangement, what meeting space looks like and what it becomes, concepts develop from allocated desks, cubicles, and offices to a hoteling concept, shared work areas, and workspace for the day, with the trade-off of fewer people in the workplace at one time. While remote work has its advantages, some duties and activities cannot be done as readily or as efficiently in a virtual environment. Conducting on-site audits and inspections, dealing with highly sensitive information, maintaining facilities and physical infrastructure, and other tasks involving the physical movement of items, people, and things are just a few examples. Furthermore, being social animals, face-to-face human connection and the formation of interpersonal relationships have an immense value that is difficult to attain in virtual contexts.

As a result, businesses should consider the future rather than a binary option between onsite and virtual. Instead, they should seek to establish flexible, adaptable workplaces where people and teams can move about as needed, depending on the nature of the work and where they and their teams are most effective.

Also, what about the new health risks that these new conceptions have spawned? Employees will have to be separated to maintain safety procedures, which may influence their sanity because too much isolation makes employees tired. As time goes on, the new office will need to become an engaging, frictionless experience for both employees and visitors. Because of the COVID-19 pandemic, we'll have to think outside the box about how we want our offices to look and how well they'll empower workers. That is the essence of the matter: if you want your employees to return to work, you must make it an appealing possibility.

As leaders begin to explore the future and where work will be performed in the future, the option should not be viewed as a binary one in which everyone either goes back to the way things were or everyone continues to do 100% telework. For a workforce that can work from anywhere but is empowered to work from where they are most effective, a more fluid—and adaptive workplace may be the best option.

PART IV

Reshaping the Nature of Work & the Workplace

Chapter 4

Leading a Thriving Hybrid Ecosystem

The Bottom Line: Adapt or become extinct. Data demonstrates an unwillingness of most people to return to the way it was. Don't look back. Reskill, move forward.

Covid-19 pandemic has accelerated the cultures and business models of firms all over the world. Organizations are attempting to thrive, with leadership bearing the brunt of the responsibilities. Simon's definition of leadership emphasizes responsibility - "Action" - rather than control. The new normal is the completely uncharted threshold for both leaders and employees, and it has resulted in a thorough rethinking of the difficulties that business leaders face. In the previous chapter, we discussed the fundamental issues that leaders face in the hybrid workplace. However, the question that needs to be answered urgently is how will enterprises navigate successfully during this period of upheaval. What do most executives do to keep their company's culture alive, maintain communication, and keep their team moving forward, as well as be proactive and get things done? As organizations adopt new ways of working at a rapid pace, Leaders are interested in transitioning to flatter, non-hierarchical structures and taking more radical methods to decision making and ways of working. The days of waiting for best practices to develop are long gone. CEOs acknowledge the need to transition from an adrenaline-based procedure during COVID-19 to a long-term approach. The winners are experimenting now, and they're doing it in a big way.

Every leadership transition creates uncertainty. Expectations are high and usually, organizations express optimism. But, Will the new leader be able to sight and seize opportunities, as well as put together the right team? Will the changes be long-term? Will there be a worthy successor? This boils down to one question: Will the leader be successful?

Why are leadership transitions so significant? A high-level executive transition is more essential than almost anything else that happens at a firm. Because of the nature of the position, a new senior leader's actions or inactivity will have a substantial impact on the company's course, for better or worse. Despite the high risks, most leaders are underprepared for — and undersupported during — the move to new responsibilities. Unlike in the past, when the transition process was informed and, in some circumstances, planned for, the recent reality of post-pandemic ushers in the unprecedented and forceful leadership transition. The ability of leaders to rise to the occasion and navigate the new normal successfully is mainly predicated on their ability to reinvent themselves in the face of uncertainty.

McKinsey senior partners Scott Keller and Mary Meaney in Leading Organization address the ten basic issues facing leaders: attracting and retaining talent, developing current talent, managing performance, creating leadership teams, making decisions, reorganizing to capture value quickly, reducing long-term overhead costs, and making culture a guiding principle. Transitional leaders must find creative approaches to handle these fundamental concerns regardless of the situation.

As leaders plan, manage, and sometimes reinvent themselves to negotiate the twists, turns, and transitions they must make, agility and adaptability are required. Making the wrong decision, on the other hand, could jeopardize a once-promising leadership career.

All things change; nothing abides. Into the same river, one cannot step twice. — Heraclitus

Changes in our leadership behaviors, competencies, attitudes, and thinking are required, if not demanded, at many periods in our jobs and careers. With the rapid transition to the hybrid workplace, how successfully we manage these potentially uncertain intersections frequently determines our eventual success — or failure — as leaders.

Whether it's a merger, acquisition, or reorganization, the development of a new product line or a shift in the competitive marketplace, or new bosses or coworkers, leaders must constantly analyze their surroundings and alter their leadership skills to match the new needs. For those who aren't nimble enough to adapt, the demand for ongoing personal change can be frightening.

We can't dispute that the consequences are massive. When asked to rank life's challenges in order of difficulty, "making a leadership transition" comes out on top, ahead of bereavement, divorce, and health problems. If the move is effective, the leader's company is likely to be successful as well; nine out of ten teams with a successful transition have met their three-year performance goals. Furthermore, such teams have a thirteen percent reduced attrition risk, a two percent greater level of discretionary effort, and a five percent higher revenue and profit than the average. However, when leaders struggle with a transition, their direct reports perform fifteen percent worse than when they work with high-performing leaders. In addition, direct reports are twenty percent more likely to be disengaged or leave the company.

Transitions, whether successful or not, incur direct costs, including advertising, searches, sign-on incentives, referral awards, and the overhead of HR experts and other executives involved. This cost is anticipated to be two hundred and thirteen percent of the annual compensation for senior executive positions. The most significant expense, though, is the loss of six, twelve, or eighteen months as the competitor moves ahead.

Without a question, leadership turnover is more common and vital than ever before. The new hybrid leaders can succeed brilliantly by focusing on the BE KNOW DO model with a People Squared Strategy.

BE KNOW DO

The United States Army developed the BE, KNOW, DO concept, which has subsequently been adopted by numerous organizations throughout the world. The model was created with military leadership practices in mind. The concept has, however, been weaved into and adapted into the global economy. Many commercial organizations nowadays have their leadership structures built around the BE KNOW DO models. BE KNOWN DO articulate the attributes of an Army leader simply and succinctly. Leadership is indeed about taking action, but there's more to it than that. Everything a leader does is based on character and competency, the BE, and the KNOW. As a result, being a leader, not just any leader, but the hybrid leader necessitates the development of all sides of one's personality. This includes embracing and demonstrating corporate ideals that benefit employees and the entire public. It also involves acquiring the characteristics and skills of a hybrid leader. Only through this process of self-improvement can you become a self-assured and capable character leader. It's not simple to be a hybrid leader in the new workplace. There are no easy answers to leadership problems, and there are no quick fixes for success. Every leader, however, has access to the tools. It is up to you to learn how to use and master it.

To be a great leader, you must model the values you expect from your employees and your company. Set a good example, be knowledgeable, and put forth the effort. Leaders cannot simply aspire to be a passive example of what they expect from their subordinates; they must absorb what they expect from their team members and live it out fully, thoroughly, and openly.

It's all about becoming the personification of both your team's fundamental principles and your company's ideals. This cannot be accomplished through the use of a mask or a suit. To have someone else work for you at all times, "even while no one is looking." For a high-quality leader, this is critical: the moral bravery to do the right thing no matter who is looking or what is going on. Moral cowardice or intellectual dishonesty has no place at the top

BE

What role does the word "BE" play in the leadership paradigm? Is there anything more profound than a surface-level, ultimately meaningless definition like "Be the change you wish to see in the world"? When it comes to leadership, I venture to say that you must be willing to go beyond a motivational quote overlaid on a stock photo on your office wall. You must not only believe in yourself, your team, your organization, and your objective, but you must also find a method to persuade others to do likewise. How do you go about doing this? Well, isn't that the million-dollar question?

Be a mentor. Be a role model. Become a motivator. Be a leader.

You must be the authority and the standard-bearer. What happens if you aren't an expert or make a mistake? Be truthful and take responsibility for your actions. Be a person of integrity, which means you must keep your promises.

Be who you say you are, and do what you say you'll do. When you make a mistake, you must have the fortitude to accept criticism, even if it is not always constructive. Challenges should not be viewed as problems to be solved, but rather as chances to learn and grow. Do whatever it takes to finish the work on schedule while remaining true to your principles, ethics, and the law.

Above all, don't be hesitant to make a decision. Own your decisions and your stance. Don't retreat from challenges, instead embrace them. Leaders take charge, which sometimes entails "embracing the suck."

Another life hack — or, to put it another way, a leader hack — is to choose a role model, someone you wish to be like. Strive to follow in his or her footsteps. To be honest, their public personalities will almost certainly be an idealized version of reality, but that's all for the better. Never set goals that are too easy to achieve. Otherwise, you're just treading water, not striving for greatness.

A character is a representation of an individual's inner power, the BE in BE, KNOW, DO. Your character not only assists you in knowing what is right, but it also relates that knowledge to action. Character gives you the courage to do the right thing no matter what the situation or the repercussions are.

Your actions show what kind of person you are. As a leader, one of your most important jobs is to instill corporate principles in your subordinates. The adage "actions speak louder than words" has never been more applicable than in this case. Leaders who preach about respect, commitment, and selfless service but do not practice these values—both on and off the job—send the wrong message, implying that all of this "values stuff" is empty rhetoric.

The first step is to learn about a company's values and leadership characteristics. You must also embrace these beliefs and leadership qualities, practicing them until they become second nature. You must instill these ideals in your subordinates via action and example, as well as assist them in developing their qualities.

KNOW

To be competent, a leader needs a particular amount of knowledge. There are four skill domains in which this knowledge is applied. Interpersonal skills, as well as an understanding of your team and how to interact with them, must be developed. To execute your job, you'll need intellectual abilities, as well as the capacity to comprehend and apply doctrine and other concepts. You'll need to pick up new soft and technical abilities, as well as learn how to use your skills effectively. Finally, hybrid leaders must master tactical skills, the capacity to make sound decisions about team tasks, and the entrenchment of new talent. They are the most crucial abilities for the leading standard of the new corporate environment, and they are reinforced by the other skills— interpersonal, conceptual, and technical.

Knowledge must be a non-negotiable For yourself and anyone you're considering elevating to a leadership position inside your company. All leaders are bound to lose any legitimacy they had in the eyes of those who should look to them for guidance if this crucial aspect is missing. This is a universal reality that applies to all times, places, and industries. To be an effective leader in the hybrid workplace, you must have the following abilities:

- Be Tech-savvy. Tech' is core to business strategy regardless of the sector and size. Technology is at the heart of corporate strategy. It affects every aspect of a business, assisting in expanding reach, enabling growth, and promoting distinctiveness from competitors. It also brings with it certain potentially high-impact, developing hazards to grapple with, such as cyber, privacy, and information risk management. For many firms, successful involvement in the digital trend necessitates a shift in how technology is represented inside leadership circles at the highest levels of their business. Moving away from the obsolete cost and technology paradigm and toward an approach centered on quantifying and controlling risks while keeping an eye on the results is required for tech-savvy leadership.

- Hybrid leadership requires the ability to cultivate innovation. Growth requires innovation, which every successful leader must not just support but also possess.

- Resourcefulness. Navigating through the minefield of the hybrid work-life needs leaders to be resourceful, given the challenges of the new normal.

- An effective leader's ability to plan is crucial. To succeed in this highly competitive hybrid workspace, regardless of the type of leader you are, you must continue strategic planning.

- The hybrid workspace requires a lot of collaboration. It's no longer a one-of-a-kind situation. To succeed in the new normal, you must be able to communicate with your coworkers and share your thoughts and ideas. Obtaining their thoughts and views about the progress of a project is critical in ensuring that they are not alienated.

- Interpersonal savvy is a skill that comes in handy in a variety of situations. Interpersonal skills are more important than ever in a leader's work when a project needs to go beyond the extent originally anticipated. Employees who are not adequately carried along would lose touch and feel ignored by the current trend of working remotely. Here, leadership means ensuring an effective stream of communication and the development of relationships between the leadership and the team members.

- The ability to communicate effectively is without a doubt the most important talent in the mixed workplace. Effective communication keeps people informed and involved, measures competency and allows for the most efficient completion of any project. Communication is the motivation that allows employees to maintain a positive work environment while also allowing them to improve.

- Encourages participation. How can you keep staff working from various remote locations motivated and productive? Leaders must make use of the humane approach to keep staff engaged without appearing to be overly nosy or overly watchful.

- One of the abilities that leaders must care about is instilling trust. You've previously read how trust is a challenge for leaders in the last chapter. Employees were formerly constrained by structural location, norms, and established ethics. They must work under the leadership's watchful eye and be tailed and toothed. In this scenario, getting the job done is non-negotiable. Now when everyone is at home or wherever they choose to stay, the leader must rely on the trust he has developed with his team to do and complete the work.

- Self-awareness is demonstrated. Effective leadership - across industries — comprises of a variety of characteristics, techniques, and talents, from winning team members' deep regard to continuously producing measurable business results. Self-awareness, on the other hand, is a feature that all leaders share. Self-awareness is frequently the first step in building emotional intelligence as a leader. As a leader, developing self-awareness will improve not only individual but also organizational performance.

- Controls ambiguity. Many of the top abilities and competencies sought after by graduate recruiters, such as communication, teamwork, and leadership, are self-explanatory. But what about ambiguity management? It may be less evident, but if you want to advance in a managerial position, it will be crucial.

The further up you go, the more likely you are to have to rely on information provided by others, which may be partial or incomplete, rather than making decisions based on your findings. That's when the capacity to deal with uncertainty comes in handy.

- Learning is nimble. Leaders and their teams must practice nimble learning as part of a broader organizational learning culture to keep up with these developments and make effective business decisions. Nimble learning is defined as a technique of gaining relevant and correct information at the right time to support critical action in a fast- environment. When unsure about the appropriate course of action, an agile learner is characterized by an openness and vulnerability to ask for guidance. They learn rapidly, are fearful of the unknown, and see all events as opportunities to learn.

- Situational Adaptability. The Situational Leadership model is adaptable. It adjusts to the current work environment as well as the organization's needs. Situational Leadership is not predicated on the leader's ability to perform a single task; rather, the leader adapts his or her management style to meet the needs of the business.

Adaptability is one of the most important aspects of Situational Leadership. To satisfy the changing needs of a business and its people, leaders must be able to switch between leadership styles. These leaders must be able to recognize when to modify their management style and what leadership strategy is best for each new paradigm.

The ability to master a variety of skills in various areas is critical to the company's success. True leadership, on the other hand, is concerned not just with what will carry the organization through today, but also with what it will require tomorrow as we approach an unexplored territory of uncertainty. You must work hard to master your job and be ready to take over responsibilities. Furthermore, as you advance in your career, you will encounter new difficulties, new ideas, and new ways of thinking and doing things. To complete your goal, you must learn to apply all of these.

Understanding basic job skills is just one aspect of the learning process. On the job, you'll pick up even more knowledge. Every day, good leaders improve their knowledge and skills. True leaders are continually seeking methods to improve their professional knowledge and skills. Dedicated corporate leaders rejoice at the chance to fill in, not because they've perfected the leadership role, but because they realize the greatest way to learn about it is to be right in the middle of it. As a result, transformational leaders will push themselves and learn by doing; also, with coaching, they will learn as much from their failures as from their achievements.

DO

Leaders take action. To offer purpose, direction, and inspiration, they pull together everything they have, everything they believe, and everything they know how to do. This means a leader must be able to put the attributes listed below into practice:

- Influencing: Making judgments, expressing those conclusions, and encouraging individuals.

- Operating: what you do to achieve your organization's immediate goals.

- Improving: what you do to improve the organization's ability to achieve current or future goals.

The three words reflect the essence of excellent leadership in their simplicity and grace. May you BE, KNOW, and DO everything you can on your amazing journey to be more than you ever imagined you could be. Dare to live up to the incredible potential you've been given. Keep going towards your life's purpose with tenacity and zeal. Always remember Washington Irving's words: "Great minds have a purpose, others have wishes."

DO should be a no-brainer, yet many leaders fall short of what should be second nature to any leader by now. First and foremost, learn to listen. Always be available twenty-four hours a day, understand your team's issues, and ask questions that will assist them in resolving them. That is how future leaders are empowered.

Above all, always follow through on what you say you'll do. You have no business becoming a leader if you can't accomplish this.

Finally, always be on time and never be afraid to take on more than your fair share of the workload. You must be willing to take on difficult tasks and complete them successfully; you cannot do this if you are late, and no one will take you seriously if they perceive you are carrying a lighter weight. And believe me when I say that people will notice both of these things, and it will cost you more credibility and authority than virtually anything else.

THE POWER OF PEOPLE

People power, our ability to collaborate with others to achieve mutually beneficial outcomes, is an important aspect of our leadership, teamwork, and human connections. Some people appear to have it, whereas others do not. In our cultural common sense, how to develop these people's power appears a little mysterious.

What are the "what" and "how" of a good leader? What is the strength of their people, and how can we learn about or strengthen it? What do we lack in our grasp of the art of leadership through people?

Common interpretations of leadership tend to focus on a leader's activities, such as "create a vision and then give people what they need to achieve it." This method of expressing leadership concentrates on the leader's activities and intended objectives but ignores how they make their interactions with others effective. How do you persuade people to adopt your vision, for example? How can you get them to take responsibility for completing it?

Taking activities that are similar to those of a leader does not always imply that you will achieve leader-like results. You must elicit the appropriate responses and activities from your audience. The issue is not so much what we do as leaders as it is the outcomes of our collective efforts. To make people's power accessible, we need to expose blind spots in our mainstream society.

"Holding the center" is crucial leadership ability. Where "center" refers to a physical state of equilibrium and the ability to choose our actions in challenging situations. When we are off-center, our activities are a result of reaction rather than a decision. I also mean the holding of intent, commitment, and caring for a future outcome when I say "center." In the face of opposition, breakdown, and surprise, we must often hold our center and connect with others to assist them to hold a common core. Internal skills to handle our anxieties, doubts, and physical emotions are the foundation of this capacity. This ability allows us to assist people with their internal states and generate a sense of resolve to act from commitment rather than reaction in the future. These talents must be learned as performance arts, not as concepts.

This leads to the concept of **People Square**. This concept is around how leadership connects and collaborates with people - employees - while introducing new abilities and strengthening existing ones to help the organization achieve its objectives. People Square is a mathematical formula that means:

Double down on people + soft skills = Advance Soft skills.

To double down on people means to tackle a problem with additional focus, energy, and resources, even if the method is deemed unwise. By channeling energy toward a clear and ambitious vision, leaders may bring hope and inspiration for the future. This should not imply putting undue pressure on employees, but rather promoting effective ways for managing employees' performance beyond expectations.

We've already established in this book that skilling isn't limited to leadership. As a result, the new hybrid workspace implies that everyone, from the CEO to the entry-level employee, will need to learn new skills to successfully navigate through the lane of uncharted working procedures. The end effect is clear: a mass of advanced skilling for both leadership and employees.

We must recognize that leadership, management, teamwork, and even communication, and relationship building are all performance arts that must be honed over time. We aspire to be effective leaders, not merely leadership scholars. Our practices, in which we exercise our internal states to enable our external acts, are the source of effective leadership. Even if we aren't conscious of it, we are already doing it. For the most part, it is a fresh focus for our attention. Mentors, coaches, leaders, and exemplars are critical in teaching us how to practice effectively and promote our development.

Collaboration is more effective when there is a sense of connection and resonance. Collaboration is a type of engagement with others in which we operate to collaborate to generate mutually beneficial outcomes. Our encounters become a game of negotiating for advantage, acting for dominance, or withdrawing for safety when we don't have shared intent.

People's power is a skill that takes time to master. It is the act of becoming more profoundly connected to our fundamental humanity and caring, and then learning to apply that to our shared vision, commitments, and actions in the world.

As stated previously in the book, as long as issues abound, there must be means to handle them. As such, we will be reviewing the new normal's difficulties and leadership approach to tackling them.

Culture Challenges

The question of how a company in the new normal, the hybrid reimagined workplace, maintains its soul is at the heart of resolving the culture challenges ushered in by the hybrid workspace.

As leaders, you must examine your Guiding Principles - your Purpose, Vision, Values, and Goals - to ensure that you are still actively traveling towards your desired destination. Don't leave it to chance; if you don't manage the culture daily, you'll wind up somewhere, but most likely not where you wanted to be.

Ways Team and Organizational Culture Management Can Be Improved in The Hybrid Environment.

Even if you don't see each other every day, you can create, build, and maintain a healthy team and corporate culture. Develop employee-led and self-managed support groups, such as:

- Culture Committees, that are self-governing and managed, and tasked with serving as a senior leader barometer to maintain a finger on the pulse of the company's heartbeat. Empower them to establish a grassroots approach to keeping the organization's culture healthy and thriving by working within the organization, within groups, and across geographic regions, using vehicles such as focus groups and town hall-style gatherings.

- Executives should create the vision, direction, and tone for what it means to be a part of the business, rather than relying on a top-down approach to setting the conditions for the firm's culture.

- Allow the culture council to grow and evolve to realize the senior leadership team's cultural vision. Use this critical aspect of protecting the company's soul, which is entrusted to emerge, leaders, top-team members, and leaders... as a learning opportunity as well as an important custodial responsibility to all.

Blended Life Balance Challenges

Because of the changing nature of work, life and work are now more than ever entwined in people's DNA. This is a new trend for both employees and executives, and it will undoubtedly become the reality of the present and future workplace. It is an issue that must be swiftly handled to maintain the effective and efficient functioning of the business, whether it is a situation never seen before or, in certain situations, a gradual change expedited by the pandemic. Rather than being corporately dressed and bound to a single workplace, employees increasingly wear pajamas in front of the camera, children contest the camera while mom is in a visual meeting, and so forth. Work and personal life are inextricably linked. So, how can leaders maintain a healthy work-life balance? As a transition leader, you must:

- Assess your present leadership competencies. Develop a new way to deal with the situation which may result in adjusting your leadership style and assess whether your degree of expertise corresponds to the present hybrid workplace environment. You must be able to empathize with your staff and be more accommodating and kind to them. Employees must be effective, and your leadership approach must be in sync with the flexibility that comes with remote work.

- Uncover the gaps between your current situation and what reality expects of you now and in the future. Due to a lack of planning and expectation, several businesses were struck hard by the epidemic and had to close their doors. But how could they possibly foresee what would happen? No one expected the virus to spread, the extent of business interruption, or the stay-at-home order, just like everyone else. All of this helps leaders understand where they are now and what the future holds for them. You must be able to see beyond the present to a future in which offices may become obsolete in almost every industry.

Performance Management Challenges

Lack of visual cues and opportunities characterize the hybrid workspace. Even when there are regulations directing work done, performance will most often be judged based on the employees' trust and discretion. Constant visual monitoring of employees' activities will undoubtedly convey distrust and exhaustion. You don't want to irritate your team, thus bear the following in mind:

- The transitioning leaders must redefine value, prioritize what matters, and invent new ways to measure performance without frequent daily visual cues to assess what counts, not what they see as activity, but what they see as impact and results.

- Leaders must face the difficulty of efficiently modifying their work procedures in a way that is in line with current realities, as well as the expectations of people and your business while maintaining a lively team and company culture.

- Gain clarity and master uncertainty so you can make better decisions today and tomorrow. Learn how to delegate more effectively and gracefully navigate the conflict between freedom and autonomy versus control and micromanagement.

- Develop greater mental and emotional agility by becoming more open. Learn to recognize and question your unconscious prejudices so that they don't become a barrier to your team and organization's success. Don't assume that just because you haven't seen them in the office means they aren't working on built-in plans and constant feedback loops that monitor progress without being pushy or controlling, as this will give the impression that you lack faith in their abilities.

Communication Challenges.

Communication is more important, but also more challenging, because of the mixed work-life situation. We know communication is now more than ever the bane of corporate success. The greatest strategy to assure productivity and achieve the company goal is to maintain a positive flow of communication with a team from diverse places. As a result, mental and emotional openness and agility are required of leaders. Learn to recognize and question your unconscious prejudices so that they don't become an impediment to your team and organization's success. Curiosity and humility are used to inspire. Develop psychological safety and trust in your team, which is a vital component of effective leadership. Be clear and empathic when communicating. Adjust your methods for greater clarity and build a strong personal brand both inside and outside your company, in the eyes of your employees, customers, and industry peers.

CHAPTER V

LEADING A THRIVING HYBRID ECOSYSTEM

CHAPTER FIVE

LEADING A THRIVING HYBRID ECOSYSTEM

The hybrid work model was not nearly as prevalent a year ago. Two-thirds of leaders are considering this new method of working now. As they shift, each company will face its own set of challenges and impediments. However, if you're eager to learn and your employees believe you're looking out for their best interests, you'll have a better chance of succeeding.

We should expect a more hybrid work environment in the future. Businesses will keep their physical offices, and employees will come in on a part-time or ad-hoc basis. This hybrid environment isn't a return to the status quo. It's a new paradigm to traverse for firms, and it comes with its own set of obstacles. 2020 should not be viewed as a blip, but rather as a turning point for business owners and leaders. Positive decisions made this year may position their companies for future competitive success, whereas hasty judgments may result in new challenges down the road. It's not just about surviving the immediate turbulence. It's all about thriving and leading.

Hybrid workplaces are nothing new. For years, several areas, such as professional services, have experimented with these models with varying degrees of success. What's new is the growing number of organizations, industries, and job levels that are exploring implementing hybrid work models, which combine remote and in-person employment. Many leaders are asking themselves, "How do we make hybrid great?" as they consider these models.

The advantages of hybrid are obvious: access to a wider pool of talent, employee flexibility, and cost savings due to less physical space. Nonetheless, the fundamental difficulty of managing team members in different situations is genuine. Middle managers are critical to negotiating this complexity.

Leaders were fast to put up tools and protocols to help employees stay safe and productive at home when lockdowns and stay-at-home orders first became a reality. Video conferencing software, workplace messaging apps, and project management tools like Asana and Trello were all included.

While these tools will undoubtedly remain ingrained in our day-to-day work, leaders must consider more than collaboration to build an efficient and effective virtual or hybrid workplace. So, how can you scale the interim solution you've devised for remote work into a full-fledged virtual or hybrid workspace? As we all struggle to get more done with less, juggling competing corporate priorities and shrinking budgets, the digital ecosystems we build to support our hybrid or remote work environments must provide the best return on investment.

Hence, it's critical to focus on redefining expectations for how work gets done for both in-office and remote workers. Clear and deliberate norms for the new work setting are the foundation for success. These norms don't merely imply that in-person work and behaviors are replicated in the hybrid paradigm. It necessitates deliberation on which practices can be maintained, which must be modified, and which must be introduced.

It is sensible to conclude that these standards or practices must be practical and address specific challenges. Do you have a problem with back-to-back meetings? Meetings should be kept to a maximum of fifty minutes. You want to give individuals the freedom to balance work and life, but you also want to make sure that others don't become stuck? Establish formal team hours with clear guidelines for responding to emails, phone calls, and messages. Once these guidelines have been created, ensure that they are followed and that the experience is uniform for both people who work together and those who work remotely.

Leaders will have to show empathy toward each member of their team regularly. So, one week, they'll join the meeting from the boardroom with the rest of the team, and the next week, they'll join remotely to see how it feels.

Technology should be used to empower executives. It was determined that providing managers with the necessary technologies to accomplish their jobs was a non-negotiable. Building trust might be tough while working remotely, but employees can more readily create trust when they stare straight at the camera when speaking. Additionally, supplemental illumination makes personnel appear more professional and personable. Managers who supply the appropriate technology and teach their employees such abilities will see their teams perform better.

Technologies are also required to assist teams in engaging and completing tasks. Setting clear expectations was as critical to the group as training managers to use these technologies to their maximum capacity. There's an ancillary advantage to empowering your middle managers to develop corporate tools for their teams. You earn their trust and assist their teams in succeeding.

Managerial roles should be redefined and managers should be trained to succeed. The only way for a hybrid model to work is for managers to be very clear about their responsibilities. "Setting the guardrails and being very, very precise about expectations. In a hybrid workplace, the greatest risk is that expectations aren't explicit from the start.

Managers can no longer be time supervisors in the hybrid environment. Instead, they'll have to manage connections, ensuring that speed and quality aren't jeopardized, and play a key role in linking people to one another and the business. This shift was already starting, but the hybrid workplace will hasten the process of preparing managers to be true people leaders.

To succeed in a hybrid remote/in-person work setting, leaders must put in a lot of effort. It's a new way of leading and thinking about their job that they can't entirely transition on their own.

This will necessitate a shift in leadership training, with a focus on more fundamental skills such as delegation, personal resiliency, and leading in the face of uncertainty. Convincing managers that change is important, and that they should want and need to change. After coaching them, give them a checklist with questions like: have you checked in with your employee, how open is your communication, how independently are they working, and so on. It's simple, but it exemplifies what they should be aiming for.

Prepare your managers to lead from a human perspective. Employees benefit from the hybrid model's flexibility. It also has the potential drawback of reducing the number of times employees have to form meaningful relationships with one another, their management, and the business. To thrive, trust is the first step.

Managers must speak openly about trust. It can be as basic as presenting a simple framework on trust at the end of a meeting and asking the team to grade themselves on it. Even bringing up the subject openly can help to build trust.

Though it's important to emphasize the significance of employee happiness. The focus on physical and mental health will continue even after the pandemic. Executives must consider how to equip middle managers to undertake difficult conversations as there will be a whole new set of issues that they may not have faced before or for which they may not have the tools.

Keep in mind that the success of hybrid begins with you. For leaders, there's much to be said for being acutely aware of the decisions you're making and considering how they could appear to others, especially if they go against the culture or messaging you're trying to promote.

Role modeling is an essential theme in the hybrid setting. People have this idea that they have to put all of their energy and time into working, working, working. When I take care of yourself and your team, you take care of your business.

Leaders must be nimble learners as well. learn new skills to manage your employees from afar. Are you mentally and technically prepared to lead, communicate, and participate in both the office and on a screen? Set an example for your team and be a change ambassador for long-term leadership. Leaders who want to lead a healthy hybrid environment must understand that sustainable leadership begins with them. Bringing it all together to produce value for future generations in your team and organization. Leaders can demonstrate how managers can care for their employees by caring for their managers, in addition to using a mantra: "We're experiencing middle management fatigue. Create room for your managers, spend time with them individually, check in on how they're doing, share some of your frustrations, and provide the coaching they require if you're a leader.

THE KEY TO BUILDING THE NEW TALENT PIPELINE

To accept a changing workplace and promote success, organizations must develop and nurture current employees' skills and leverage them across the organization in new ways. While employees learn new skills and are exposed to new technology, the post-COVID-19 world is an important place to start. Many firms lack insight into the skills they will need to prosper and adapt in a post-COVID environment, as the pandemic accelerates the future of work through digitization, disruption, and automation.

According to a new McKinsey Global Survey on future labor needs, nearly nine out of ten executives and managers believe their companies are either experiencing or will have skill gaps in the next five years. The World Economic Forum's Future of Jobs Report, COVID-19 is expected to displace eighty-five million jobs across fifteen industries and twenty-six economies. Simultaneously, ninety-seven million new jobs might be created, better suited to the new labor divide between humans, machines, and algorithms.

Workers and organizations today require substantially different attributes to survive and succeed than they did in the past; many of the future's positions, skills, and job titles are unknown. Critical thinking, emotional intelligence, and teamwork are becoming increasingly important, and firms that do not consider these talent pipeline requirements are at risk.

In today's world, new ways of working are profoundly changing the talent management function. This is not the time to sit back and wait for things to happen. Businesses that wish to keep up in the competition to be tomorrow's workplace must put technology on the agenda today and follow these guidelines:

- **Multi-Tiered Approach**

Leaders can use the hybrid workplace to restructure existing office layouts, recruit fresh talent from different parts of the country, and diversify their workforce. Companies have also noticed a favorable influence on employee satisfaction and productivity as a result of remote working. The hybrid environment is a means of sustaining that good impact over time. In this aspect, leaders must avoid being too strict while allowing for a multi-tier strategy that will allow the hybrid ecology to thrive. As a result, the following should be taken into account:

- Emerging Leaders

You might be considering a hybrid approach to work, in which people work both remotely and in the office, now that many companies are reopening offices. In terms of assets, logistics, policies, and leadership, there's a lot to sort out. A mixed work environment necessitates a new leadership style as well as new abilities. You and your fellow leaders must adapt your leadership style to the situation.

What I mean is that with hybrid work, the social functions of a physical office become more important, but when employees are distant, procedures and processes take precedence. As a leader, you must be able to switch back and forth between the two environments and facilitate both types of work. It should not be the same old leadership style and approach.

Plan time in the office for teams to undertake collaborative work that is best done by individuals, such as brainstorming or prototyping. And, whether it's hosting happy hours or offering yoga lessons, create activities and events that bring people together casually and socially.

Promote relationship development by ensuring that people meet people they would not ordinarily meet and that new people have the opportunity to hang out with and get to know others. Also, allow people to interact socially. When employees are in the office, avoid scheduling back-to-back meetings. Consider scheduling no-meeting time on everyone's calendars if required. Encourage employees to leave their desks and interact with one another. The best way to encourage employees to socialize is to socialize yourself. Make yourself available for people to approach you informally rather than locking yourself away in a locked office. Participate in social gatherings and activities, and strike up non-work conversations on the spur of the moment.

Flex to a different leadership style when it comes to remote work. Allowing others to get things done and succeed should be your priority. This can be accomplished through access, standards, and engagement.

Ensure that everyone working remotely has access to the tools and resources they require to be productive. Consider one of the numerous innovative communication and collaboration systems that allow people in various time zones or on different work schedules to work together asynchronously. Establish guidelines for live interactions, such as meetings and one-on-ones, to ensure that they are relevant, actionable, and efficient.

Also, make certain that everyone is involved. In a remote scenario, people are less likely to speak up, and nuances can be lost, so utilize active listening and proactively elicit input, questions, and comments. Also, manage visibility to engage people. I mean, manage other people's visibility by ensuring that everyone, not just those who spend more time in the office, gets contacted, invited to opportunities, and is informed about what's going on. And keep your visibility up by being available when and how people need you, assisting people individually based on their needs, and keeping track of how everyone is doing and the results they're achieving.

Hybrid work has both advantages and disadvantages. Take advantage of the differences between working in an office and working remotely, and adapt your leadership style to the situation.

- Leading others

Your employees' requirements are constantly changing. However, as many firms prepare to return to the office in some form or another, your team members are likely to be in a variety of scenarios. Some have limited or no daycare or manage their children's online education; others have health difficulties that prevent them from returning to in-person work, and yet others are eager to leave the house and return to their workstations. How do you manage these varying circumstances as a leader while treating everyone fairly? What protocols can you put in place to ensure that office personnel and those working from home are on the same page? How can you maintain flexibility when plans can alter at any time? And how do you assist your employees in coping with their stress levels during this period of transition?

It will be extremely difficult to please everyone once an official hybrid policy is adopted. Following such a trying year, most businesses adopted a more human-centered strategy, emphasizing empathy as the most important aspect in building effective employee connections. However, catering to each individual's unique demands would be challenging without encountering some pushback

Should one employee's request to work from home on a mandated in-office day be reviewed on an individual basis? Will this be seen as unjust by other employees?

If firms want to ensure a seamless hybrid adoption, managers must pay increased attention to and evaluate these topics. Many leaders, on the other hand, are portraying the change as a high-stakes game of trial and error.

- Managing Team

You'd like to gather your team for a quick brainstorming session. You might have popped your head out of the office a few years back and invited everyone to grab a snack and join you in the conference room. Today? Things aren't exactly as straightforward as they appear.

As you prepare to return to work, you realize that you may have a few employees who are working on, a few who have chosen to work totally from home, and a few who do both.

For leaders, this creates several questions. How will they ensure that everyone is on the same page? When people aren't together, how can they promote a positive team culture? Will they end up bouncing back and forth like a wayward ping-pong ball between their in-office and remote teams?

Managing a hybrid team can be intimidating, but don't worry: it's achievable. Let's look at what you need to know to keep your entire staff happy and productive, no matter where they work.

Here's the next question you're probably thinking about: How do you gain the benefits of leading a hybrid team while still avoiding all of the pitfalls?

Recognize that this is a learning process, to begin with. For many managers, hybrid teams are unfamiliar ground, so expect some bumps along the way. That's fine as long as you're willing to learn from them.

Here are a few more techniques to assist you to manage a hybrid team in this new world of work now that you've shown yourself some well-deserved grace and patience.

- Encourage a remote-first mindset.

- Have faith in your employees to deliver on their promises.

- Offer and solicit feedback regularly. 4. Provide opportunities for social interaction.

- Make sure your entire team is on the same page (Without Actually Being Together)

- **Leading function**

While hybrid work offers employees a lot of freedom and allows organizations to have an energetic office environment, it also raises some serious leadership issues. How can you support your team's growth in a hybrid environment? How do you strike a balance between in-person and virtual team members? How can you ensure those who call into meetings have the same opportunity to contribute as those who are present in the meeting room? When informal interactions are limited, how can you create relationships with remote employees? How can you ensure that remote employees are considered for the same opportunities as in-office employees, even if they are not present? When informal interactions are limited, how can you create relationships with remote employees? How can you ensure that remote employees are considered for the same opportunities as in-office employees, even if they are not present? In a hybrid environment, how does onboarding differ? To set your team up for success, what operational policies do you need to examine, update, or implement?

- How do you feel about hybrid work? Is it possible for employees to select between virtual and in-office work? Will all employees be required to work some in-office hours?

- How can you ensure that a critical mass of employees is present in the office at the same time, allowing for the development of working relationships and the development and maintenance of business culture?

- What are the qualities that your applicants are looking for? Will the flexible working choices you provide have an impact on your talent pool?

- How much space does the company currently require? Will downsizing make you regret it later?

- Is it necessary for all employees to have their own office space, or could "hoteling" or collaborative workplaces be a better option?

- **Leading Business Strategy**

Many businesses make quick and ill-advised decisions due to a lack of study and planning, thereby impacting their enterprise value. Our need for simplicity should not trump our need for thoroughness, especially when a company's future is at stake.

Many CEOs have been seduced by easy-to-use strategic templates that produce a quick-and-dirty corporate strategy in a world where they are overcaffeinated, stressed, and time-starved. Downloading a template, on the other hand, encourages short-sighted thinking and poorly executed techniques. The end outcome is frequently something more like a tactical plan than a true strategy.

- Create a clear vision

- Identify your competitive advantage.

- Establish your objectives

- Concentrate on long-term development.

- Make decisions based on facts.

- Be nimble, but think long-term.

- Be open-minded.

- **Overcoming The Skill Displacement**

The shift to a remote and hybrid workplace has changed the way businesses operate. It also brought attention to the talents required for the position. The mix of abilities required to succeed in the digital workplace was under scrutiny even before the rise of remote and hybrid working practices.

The advent of remote and hybrid employment necessitated a change in goals and expenditure. However, there are still many unanswered questions: How do you strike a balance between hard technical abilities like coding and project management and "soft skills" like influencing and communication? What are the practical steps that employees can take to improve these skills? Organizations that want to adopt a hybrid working model must upgrade their current skills to match their office layout and the rapidly changing needs of consumers to keep up with industry changes.

Determine the skills employees will need in a hybrid workforce. Examine existing training modules and change any areas that do not lead to the future cementing of your hybrid work arrangement. Leading hybrid teams requires agility and flexibility, therefore look for abilities that can assist your team in achieving these qualities. You may teach your employees how to use data and analytics, artificial intelligence, and machine learning. Although a mixed work setup appears to be the way of the future, there are still obstacles to overcome. According to the data, sixty percent of polled business leaders are concerned about productivity, which makes them reconsider using telecommuting.

- **The New Employee Social Contract**

For many years, the social contract between employers and employees was that the latter would labor for the corporation in exchange for compensation. Then it was supplemented with additional advantages such as health insurance and a provident fund. The modern social contract between employers and employees has altered over the last few years, partly as a result of the entrance of new generations – Gen Y and Gen Z – into the workplace, and partly as a result of technological advancements. This social compact has undergone new alterations as a result of the pandemic, and various intangible aspects have become a part of it.

The younger generation must believe in the company's vision, mission, and aim, as well as social responsibility, to work. They will only choose to work for a company that believes in them and can help them advance in their careers by providing opportunities for growth and learning. Another element added to the social contract is employee well-being; the rush to pay for immunization for employees and their families among Indian corporations is proof of this. A lot has changed, even from the perspective of an organization. Companies are aware that their HR departments must now regard their employees as internal clients and provide round-the-clock service.

Employees also feel the need to be recognized and appreciated more frequently in the social contract. As a result, executives should strive to recognize and promote those employees who have excelled during the remote-working phase. People struggled to manage their time in the early days of the remote-working period. Certain firms have begun to draw a line between work and personal life in various ways, which has aided in the smooth operation of the remote work culture. It is true that some employees, particularly those in charge of international operations, work longer than expected. However, how much employees are recognized and rewarded is entirely dependent on the reporting managers and the firm standards placed on them.

With the introduction of technology, work-life has penetrated the living room, unlike in the past. While remote working is not new, the epidemic has brought its benefits to the forefront, necessitating a shift in the social approach to the employee-employer relationship. There are still some functions that cannot be performed remotely, but businesses are making progress in every area they can. In the post-pandemic era, technology and emotional quotient play a significant role in the social contract between the two parties. Nobody could have predicted that these two would find their way into the social contract, written or unwritten.

- **The Workforce And Leadership Composition Of Today The Future**

The hybrid workforce is built on new skills, adaptability, diversity, and a hybrid–blended life balance (work-life balance). One of the most difficult business issues of our day is navigating the pandemic and its aftermath. Most businesses adopted new ways of working to keep operations running, which resulted in idle offices, factories, and storefronts.

More than a year later, the world has changed dramatically. As the economy recovers, management teams are tasked with guiding their organizations through these rapid transitions. Boards of directors are also important. They must assist management in critically considering the formulation and implementation of return-to-work strategies. Understanding the workforce problems executives confront in a post-pandemic world is the first step, as it allows them to ask the proper questions and serve as a sounding board.

Leadership quality has been revealed to be a significant factor of an organization's success in recent research, which explains why firms are investing more in leadership-focused projects. Strong leaders lead to improved overall organizational performance, including increased customer happiness, organizational productivity, financial gains, and product quality. Employee retention, performance, engagement, and morale all benefit from effective leadership.

In summary, today's and tomorrow's leaders will need a different set of talents than those of the past. They must have great leadership abilities in addition to being specialists in their respective fields of work to effectively manage their teams. Here's a look at the skills they'll need, why they're vital, and how to improve them. Large-scale shifts are affecting how people operate and how business gets done." "Leaders who effectively adapt to these trends may ensure that their companies stand out from the competition.

FAILURE TO ADAPT

Leaders will withdraw into their comfort zones as organizations return to work, welcoming going back to the office while keeping the usual method in the back of their thoughts. For any leader, this is a very risky route to take. Adaptability can, and should, be cultivated in this period of rapid change. Self-care, a focus on purpose, the ability to detect the default mindset, deeper connections with colleagues, and a safe learning environment is all necessary for developing the adaptation muscle.

The COVID-19 pandemic provided an opportunity to reassess our approach to work. It's a paradigm shift that happens just once every generation and has the power to influence society in numerous ways. As leaders, companies, and people battle with learning best practices, testing solutions and accepting that no one has all the answers, McKinsey highlighted the need for humility this week.

If companies refuse to address the gap between how employers and their employees perceive the future, they risk alienating—and perhaps losing—their workforce. Employers seek to restore normalcy by getting employees back to work; employees want far more work-from-home opportunities. The stakes are high for companies: according to recent surveys, 40% of workers worldwide are considering leaving their current employers before the end of the year. Companies must accept that developing a hybrid working paradigm will be a long-term endeavor that will necessitate extensive testing and learning.

As a result, the concept of holding our meetings in a more formal setting – with no children, dogs, food, or drinks (since people value the authenticity and transparency that Covid has imposed on us) – should be scrapped. It's acceptable to be real, to be human, and that means acknowledging that we all used to have a dual life (ourselves at work And ourselves at home; now we can be our true selves, and that's fine.) It's like that commercial when the mother moves around in her seat to cover her child jumping in and out of her video meeting. As a result, forcing staff back in the old ways will be a huge disservice. That is something we should not have to do.

Leaders were unprepared for and failed to master their new talents, similar to being thrown into the deep end of a pool — they doggy paddled to the side but did not learn to swim. As the findings show, firms are unable to take advantage of technological potential due to skill and knowledge shortages. Moreover, because skill disparities exist across the global labor market, hiring a distributed workforce to bridge the talent gap is no longer the best answer.

Why would anyone want to go back to the way things were before after experiencing the setback of not adjusting to the hybrid environment of the new normal? What is the true motivator? Comfort – It's simple — it's well-known. It's a sign of a lack of adaptation, agility, and change management. And if leaders fail to consider new styles and approaches, the consequences can be severe.

Failure to adapt to the hybrid ecosystem will result in:

- The majority of skilled employees are leaving, which will cost the company time and money in the future. Additional obstacles may arise as a result of the fast-paced environment, limited funds, and uncertainty regarding future skills requirements. It doesn't imply, though, that you can't come up with a clever performance management strategy to keep your top performers.

Talents will be dissatisfied and seek better possibilities if your strategy reskilling and performance management do not coincide with ongoing, personalized talent development that is focused on each individual's performance. You'll be on the hook for the bill. As a result, you'll need data and technology that work together to precisely measure your workforce's progress so that you can provide relevant learning and business activities that are critical for your company's and industry's further growth. You don't need to rush to acquire future skillsets if you're constantly assessing and growing them now, putting knowledge into practice as soon as possible.

You will gain long-term benefits in the form of an in-house talent pool and a hefty ROI if you invest in the right performance management tools. You will not only improve your current workforce productivity by upskilling them, but you will also gain long-term benefits in the form of an in-house talent pool and a hefty ROI if you invest in the right performance management tools.

- Attracting talent will become cutthroat and competitive, similar to the large sign-on bonuses offered in the late 1980s and 1990s when Silicon Valley's Internet Startups were launching. In terms of talent management and team morale, we must evaluate what will happen if your company continues down the standard office work environment road in the future.

While this is undoubtedly necessary for some firms and positions, there is reason to assume that increasing flexibility for all employees, regardless of company size, industry, or role, would be beneficial. The employment market is becoming more competitive, and firms may now hire from a variety of talent pools that were previously unreachable, thanks to the rise of remote and hybrid work opportunities around the world.

For organizations that have temporarily shifted to work from home and are considering a return to the office, your team members' attitudes may differ substantially. Overall, regardless of industry, if you want to remain competitive as an employer of choice, you'll need to provide possibilities for your staff to embrace flexible working through a hybrid strategy.

- Apathy at the core of the workforce and among front-line – middle management, where the work is done in a firm, is being caused by new levels of motivation. We can rethink our performance measurement with the hybrid model. Leaders have always desired to have as many of their workers present in the workplace as possible, ensuring hours worked and increasing efficiency. Project management would be viewed via the lens of "hours inputted."

With some employees working remotely, it's more critical than ever to know who's directly responsible for what project and how much they can do in a day. The focus for management shifts to increasing productivity, which includes providing teammates with the tools they require and scoping tasks in a logical order. Much about how we work has been upended by the pandemic, and what follows next is neither the death of the office nor a restoration to the status quo. Instead, we will collaborate with employees who are co-located in the same physical space as well as colleagues who work remotely in our new reality.

Hybridity combines the advantages of remote work (more flexibility, lower carbon footprint, lower labor costs, and higher employee satisfaction) with the critical qualities of traditional, co-located work (smoother coordination, informal networking, stronger cultural socialization, greater creativity, and face-to-face collaboration). Managers must be aware of the power dynamics at play to realize the many benefits of hybrid working. To avoid demotivating their interest and trust in the organization's culture, they must gain knowledge of hybridity positioning and hybridity competence, as well as take steps to level the playing field for their teams.

Notes

Chapter 1

1. Aschauer, D. A. (1989). Is Public Expenditure Productive? Journal of Monetary Economics, 23(2),177–200. doi10.1016/0304-3932(89)90047-0; and Hayaloğlu
2. Brian Wang, "$160 billion hedge fund wants artificial intelligence software to make 75% of all management decisions by 2022," NextBigFuture, December 16, 2016.
3. Cherry K., (2020) The Democratic Style of Leadership. https://www.verywellmind.com/what-is-democratic-leadership-2795315
4. Congressional Research Service; Global Economic Effects of COVID-19. July 9, 2021.
5. Gerald C. Kane, Doug Palmer, Anh Nguyen Phillips, David Kiron, and Natasha Buckley, Achieving digital maturity: Adapting your company to a changing world, Deloitte University Press, July 13, 2017.
6. ING, "Agile working," accessed January 22, 2018.
7. Jerlin Huang's; The Evolution of Work: The Who, What and Where. (https://medium.com/the-innovation-market/the-evolution-of-work-75dd91a55a9a)
8. Jacob Morgan's; The Evolution Of Work. (https://www.forbes.com/sites/jacobmorgan/2013/09/10/the-evolution-of-work/?sh=4cc6bc80679e)
9. Jeff Schwartz, Laurence Collins, Heather Stockton, Darryl Wagner, and Brett Walsh, The future of work: The augmented workforce, Deloitte University Press, February 28, 2017.

10. Jelmer W. Eerkens, Kevin J. Vaughn, and John Kantner; The Evolution of Leadership. 2010.

11. Judit Kapás; Industrial Revolutions and the Evolution of Firm Organization. Economic Growth, Development, and Institutions – Lessons for Policy and the Need for an Evolutionary Framework of Analysis", November 1-3, 2007, Porto.

12. Khan S. M., et al., (2015) The Style of Leadership: A Critical Review https://iiste.org/Journals/index.php/PPAR/article/view/20878

13. Lawrence F. Katz and Alan B. Krueger, The rise and nature of alternative work arrangements in the United States, 1995–2015, National Bureau of Economic Research working paper no. 22667, September 2016.

14. Mikal Khoso, "How much data is produced every day?," Level blog, Northeastern University; Tom Davenport and David Rosner, Decoding the path to purchase: Using autonomous analytics for customer mapping, Deloitte University Press, November 11, 2016.

15. Oliver Ralph, "Businesses set targets for recruiting older workers," Financial Times, May 23, 2017.

16. Pınar. (2015). The Impact of Developments in the Logistics Sector on Economic Growth: The Case of OECD Countries. International Journal of Economics and Financial Issues. 5. 523-530.Jennie Dusheck, "Stanford Medicine, Google team up to harness power of data science for health care," News Center, accessed November 5, 2017.

17. Stacey Philpot and Kelly Monahan, "A data-driven approach to identifying future leaders," MIT Sloan Management Review, summer 2017.

18. Serebrisky, T. (2014) Sustainable infrastructure for competitiveness and inclusive growth, IDB

19. Reuters, "UBS is giving its investment bankers two hours of 'personal time' every week," Fortune, June 2, 2016123.

20. Roy Maurer, Using data to make better hires, Society for Human Resource Management, January 29, 2016.

21. Sonny Chheng, Kelly Monahan, and Karen Reid, "Beyond office walls and balance sheets: Culture and the alternative workforce,"

Deloitte Review 21, Deloitte University Press, July 31, 2017. Deloitte WikiStrat report, 2017.

22. Stanley Aibieyi, (2014). Approaches, Skills And Styles Of Leadership In Organizations; A Review of Public Administration and Management Vol. 3, No. 5, July 2014.

23. Wilde A., How Leadership Impacts Employee Performance https://www.jazzhr.com/blog/how-leadership-impacts-employee-performance/

24. World Bank Group; Infrastructure financing in times of COVID-19: A driver of recovery. July 24, 2020.

25. Yılmaz, Derya & Cetin, Isin. (2018). The Impact of Infrastructure on Growth in Developing Countries: Dynamic Panel Data. Analysis

Chapter 2

1. Julie Kniseley; How to Foster Company Culture in Today's "New Normal" (https://www.jmco.com/how-to-foster-company-culture-todays-new-normal/).

2. Sammy Rubin (2021). Employees Want More From Their Workplaces Post-Pandemic — Here's How To Get Started. Forbe. Jun 18, 2021, U.S. Chamber of Commerc; The Dynamic Office of Tomorrow: 3 Future Workplace Trends. June 29, 2021

3. International Finance Corporation. How Firms are Responding and Adapting During COVID-19 and Recovery; OPPORTUNITIES FOR ACCELERATED INCLUSION IN EMERGING MARKETS: March, 2021.

4. Lauren Thomas (2021). Covid changed how we think of offices. Now companies want their spaces to work as hard as they do. Published Wed, Mar 10 2021 11:23 Am Est updated Wed, Mar 10 2021 12:46 Pm Est. (Tom Spiggle (2020). Coronavirus Silver Lining: A Better Work-Life Balance? Forbes. Oct 14, 2020, 01:22pm.

5. Kumanu, Defining Work-Life Balance: Energy is the Missing Ingredient. (https://www.kumanu.com/defining-work-life-balance-its-history-and-future/).

6. Authors' calculations based on data from GSMA Intelligence, quarterly growth rates during 2019. See: GSMA. 2020. "The

7. Mobile Gender Gap Report 2020. https://www.gsma.com/mobilefordevelopment/wp-content/uploads/2020/02/GSMA-The Mobile-Gender-Gap-Report-2020.pdf

8. Economist. 2020. "The Pandemic Is Liberating Firms to Experiment with Radical New Ideas." April 25, 2020. https://www.economist.com/business/2020/04/25/the-pandemic-is-liberating-firms-to-experiment-with-radical-new-ideas

9. Economist. 2020. "Why Voting Online Is Not the Way to Hold an Election in a Pandemic." April 28, 2020. https://www.economist.com/international/2020/04/27/why-voting-online-is-not-the-way-to-hold-an-election-in-a-pandemic. See: World Economic Forum and Global Challenge Insight Report: "The Future of Jobs" Employment, Skills and Workforce Strategy for the Fourth Industrial Revolution. 2016.

10. Boston Consulting Group, Man and Machine in Industry 4.0: How Will Technology Transform the Industrial Workforce Through 2025? 2015.

11. Industrial Global Union, Industry 4.0 the industrial revolution happening now, 4 December 2015, www.industriall-union.org/industry-40-theindustrial-revolution-happening-now.

12. O'Connor, S., "The human cloud: A new world of work", Financial Times, 8 October 2015.

13. International Labour Organisation (ILO), World Economic and Social Outlook 2015, 2015.

14. Brynjolfsson, E. and A. McAfee, The Second Machine Age: Work, Progress, and Prosperity in a Time of Brilliant Technologies, 2014.

15. Annunziata, M. and S. Biller, The Future of Work, GE Discussion Paper, General Electric, 2014.

16. Frey, C. and M. Osborne, The Future of Employment: How Susceptible are Jobs to Computerisation? Oxford Martin School Programme on the Impacts of Future Technology, September 2013.
17. Lame the Robots: Assessing the Job Polarization Explanation of Growing Wage Inequality, Economic Policy Institute and Center for Economic Policy Research Working Paper, 2013.
18. McKinsey Global Institute, Disruptive technologies: Advances that will transform life, business, and the global economy, 2013.

Chapter 3

1. Rita Zeidner is a freelance writer based in Falls Church, Va. (https://www.shrm.org/hr-today/news/all-things-work/pages/remote-work-has-become-the-new-normal.aspx)
2. Brian Westfall (2021). Overcoming the 5 Biggest Challenges of Managing Remote Employees. (https://www.softwareadvice.com/resources/challenges-managing-remote-employees/)
3. Howard Spira (2021). New normal: Emergent jealousy and other challenges for leaders in a post-COVID world. (https://federalnewsnetwork.com/commentary/2021/03/new-normal-emergent-jealousy-and-other-challenges-for-leaders-in-a-post-covid-world/)
4. Barbara Z. Larson, et Al(2020). A Guide to Managing Your (Newly) Remote Workers. (https://hbr.org/2020/03/a-guide-to-managing-your-newly-remote-workers)
5. Rachel S. Cohen, "Air Force vice chief: Nearly one-third of employees may permanently telework," Air Force Magazine, September 16, 2020; Scott Maucione, "'We're not going back,' Air Force leadership says telework is here to stay," Federal News Network, September 16, 2020.
6. Megan Brenan, "COVID-19 and remote work: An update," Gallup, October 13, 2020.

7. Fiorella Riccobono, "1 in 2 professionals dread work every morning," Team Blind blog, August 7, 2020. This is from analysis of responses to the Deloitte Human Insights Survey, including responses from public and private sector respondents.

8. Jim Harter, "Employee engagement on the rise in the U.S.," Gallup, August 26, 2018.

9. United States Office of Personnel Management, Federal work-life survey: Governmentwide report, March 2018.

10. U.S. Senate Committee on Environment and Public Works, Global workplace analytics, July 27, 2020.

11. Fastco Works, "The upside of a flexible work week," Fast Company, October 11, 2020.

12. Phil Goldstein, "How federal agencies expanded their telework environments," FedTech, October 19, 2020;

13. Tom Temin, "The future of telework at Homeland Security," Federal News Network, August 27, 2020; Eric Katz, "Extolling productivity during pandemic, agencies say they'll make some telework permanent," Government Executive, November 18, 2020. 127

14. Nicola Band; Are Blended team the new post-covid 19 'normal?' (https://futureworx.io/are-blended-workforce-teams-the-new-post-covid-19-normal/)

15. HR Grapevine; Workforce| Leadership and Coaching is set to become the 'new normal.' (https://www.hrgrapevine.com/content/article/2020-09-22-leadership-coaching-is-set-to-become-the-new-normal)

16. Joseph Folkman. Are your employees at home actually working? 5 Behaviors that indicate productivity to managers. (https://www.forbes.com/sites/joefolkman/2020/07/07/are-your-employees-at-home-actually-working-5-behaviors-that-indicate-productivity-to-managers/?sh=21c23c116b5f)

Chapter 4

1. Rich Lesser et Al. (2021): Leading Through the Big Transition: BCG Publication. (https://www.bcg.com/publications/2021/preparing-business-leaders-for-a-post-covid-19-era)
2. The Epoch Team. Chris Erickson (2019): The Be Do Know Model of Leadership. (https://medium.com/@annikajiajia/the-be-know-do-model-of-leadership-6455579e152d)
3. Scott Keller (2018): Successfully transitioning to new leadership roles. McKinsey publication. (https://www.mckinsey.com/business-functions/organization/our-insights/successfully-transitioning-to-new-leadership-roles).
4. Neil Grimmer (2017): How to Sell Your Company Without Destroying Its Soul. (https://www.entrepreneur.com/article/296813)
5. Bob Dubham 2014: In The Peoples Power of Effective Leaders. (https://generateleadership.com/blog/power-of-effective-leaders/)
6. Christine M. Riordan (2008): In Navigating Through Leadership Transitions: Making It Past The Twists And Turns. Ivey Business Journal. (https://iveybusinessjournal.com/publication/navigating-through-leadership-transitions-making-it-past-the-twists-and-turns/)
7. Douglas MacArthur: A Soldier Speaks: Public Papers and Speeches of General of the Army Douglas MacArthur, ed. Vorin E. Whan Jr. (New York: Frederick A. Praeger, Publishers, 1965), 354, 356.
8. Lawton Collins: in The Infantry School Quarterly (April 1953): 30.
9. Edward C. Meyer: in The Chiefs of Staff, United States Army: On Leadership and the Profession of Arms (Pentagon, Washington, D.C.: The Information Management Support Center, 24 March 1997), 10 (hereafter referred to as Chiefs of Staff).
10. "The Creed of the Noncommissioned Officer": TC 22-6, The Army Noncommissioned Officer Guide, (23 November 1990), inside front cover (hereafter cited as TC 22-6).
11. COL Chamberlain at Gettysburg: John J. Pullen, The Twentieth Maine (1957; reprint, Dayton, Ohio: Press of Morningside Bookshop, 1980), 114-125 (hereafter cited as Pullen); "The Alabamians drove

the Maine men…": Geoffrey C. Ward, The Civil War: An Illustrated History (New York: Knopf, 1990), 220 (hereafter cited as Ward).

12. Douglas E. Murray: in ARMY Magazine 39, no. 12 (December 1989): 39. "More than anything else…": TRADOC Pam 525-100-2, Leadership and Command on the Battlefield: Battalion and Company (Fort Monroe, Va., 10 June 1993), 43 (hereafter cited as TRADOC Pam 525-100-2).

13. George C. Marshall: in Selected Speeches and Statements of General of the Army George C. Marshall, ed. H.A. DeWeerd (Washington, D.C.: The Infantry Journal, 1945), 176.

14. Small Unit Leaders' Initiative in Normandy: Stephen Ambrose, D-Day June 6, 1944: The Climactic Battle of World War II (New York: Simon & Schuster, 1994), 235-36 (hereafter cited as Ambrose, D-Day); "This certainly wasn't the way…": Sam Gibbons memoir (New Orleans: Eisenhower Center, University of New Orleans (hereafter cited as Eisenhower Center)).

15. "When I became Chief of Staff…": Edward C. Meyer, "A Return to Basics," Military Review 60, no. 4 (July 1980): 4.

16. George Bush: in Quotes for the Military Writer/Speaker (Department of the Army: Chief of Public Affairs, 1989), 6 (hereafter cited as Military Quotes 1989).129

Chapter 5

5 Hybrid Work Challenges & Tips to Fix Them. Hybrid Workplace. February 04, 2021. (https://www.workinsync.io/5-hybrid-work-challenges-tips-to-fix-them/)

Avery Blank: 6 Easy Steps To Overcome The Skills Gap And Advance Your Career. Forbes. September 26, 2017. (https://www.forbes.com/sites/averyblank/2017/09/26/6-easy-steps-to-overcome-the-skills-gap-and-advance-your-career/?sh=6fe97aac4561)

Corporate Learning Network. Why We Need to Focus on Leadership in the Hybrid Environment.

(https://www.corporatelearningnetwork.com/leadership-management/articles/why-we-need-to-focus-on-leadership-in-the-hybrid-environment)
Denise Lee Yohn. Hybrid leadership for hybrid work: SmartBrief. April 13, 2021. (https://www.smartbrief.com/original/2021/04/hybrid-leadership-hybrid-work)
Graduate Programs Staff. Top 5 Leadership Skills for the Workplace of Tomorrow. Northeastern University Graduate Program, September 4, 2019. (https://www.northeastern.edu/graduate/blog/essential-leadership-skills-for-tomorrow/)
Greg Tigges: How to Thrive in a Hybrid Work Environment. LinkedIn. June 10, 2021. (https://www.linkedin.com/pulse/how-thrive-hybrid-work-environment-greg-tigges)
John Brownridge. Digital workplaces and the hybrid work model: Reimagining digital workplaces for hybrid work environments. July 19, 2021. (https://www2.deloitte.com/us/en/blog/human-capital-blog/2021/digital-workplace-and-the-hybrid-work-model.html).
Jodi Cachey: How to Build a Tech Ecosystem that Supports Remote Work. RingCentral. April 20, 2021. (https://www.ringcentral.co.uk/gb/en/blog/how-to-build-a-tech-ecosystem-that-supports-remote-work/).
Kevin Sneader and Bob Sternfels: From surviving to thriving: Reimagining the post-COVID-19 return: Mckinsey & Company. May 1, 2020. (https://www.mckinsey.com/featured-insights/future-of-work/from-surviving-to-thriving-reimagining-the-post-covid-19-return)
Kat Boogaard: How To Successfully Manage A Hybrid Model Team. Trello. February 19, 2021. (https://blog.trello.com/manage-a-hybrid-model-team)
Marc Emmer: 10 steps to building a killer business strategy you can execute flawlessly. Vintage. July 1, 2020. (https://www.vistage.com/research-center/business-leadership/strategic-planning/20181105-10-steps-building-best-business-strategies/).
Mackay's Paul. Why you will lose the war on talent if you don't embrace hybrid work: Pragmatic Thinking. (https://pragmaticthinking.com/blog/lose-the-war-on-talent-if-you-dont-embrace-hybrid-work/)
Mark Mortensen and Martine Haas. Making the Hybrid Workplace Fair: Harvard Business Review. Leadership And Managing People, February 24, 2021. (https://hbr.org/2021/02/making-the-hybrid-workplace-fair)

Ned Wasniewski: Leading In A Hybrid Work Environment. Insightful Experience. (https://blog.insight-experience.com/leading-in-a-hybrid-work-environment)

Parag Patki: Using technology to form a talent pipeline. Inside He. February 26, 2021. (https://www.insidehr.com.au/form-a-talent-pipeline/).

Sudeshna Mitra | HRKatha - What's the new social contract between employees and employers. March 30, 2021. (https://www.hrkatha.com/features/whats-the-new-social-contract-between-employees-and-employers/)

Scott Clark. Top Skills for the Hybrid and Digital Workplace. July 26, 2021. (https://www.reworked.co/digital-workplace/top-skills-for-the-hybrid-and-digital-workplace/)

Steve Hogarty. What is the hybrid workplace model? WeWork Ideas. April 1, 2021. (https://www.wework.com/ideas/workspace-solutions/flexible-products/hybrid-workplace)

The post-pandemic workforce: what boards should be thinking about. (https://www.pwc.com/us/en/services/governance-insights-center/library/covid-19-returning-workplace-boards.html).

Tracy Ring: How to Encourage Your Team to Survive and Thrive in a Hybrid Environment. July 12, 2021. (https://www.outbackteambuilding.com/blog/survive-and-thrive-in-a-hybrid-environment/)

Tineke A. Keesmaat: 5 Ways Leaders Can Support Their Middle Managers in a Hybrid Workplace. LinkedIn. February 9, 2021. (https://www.linkedin.com/pulse/5-ways-leaders-can-support-middle-managers-hybrid-tineke-a-keesmaat)

Tomas Chamorro-Premuzic and Reece Akhtar: 3 Traits You Need to Thrive in a Hybrid Work Environment. Harvard Business Review. August 03, 2021. (https://hbr.org/2021/08/3-traits-you-need-to-thrive-in-a-hybrid-work-environment)

Made in the USA
Monee, IL
01 October 2021

79186847R00079